MY HOME'S IN MONTANA

By Kareen Bratt

ISBN-10: 146-1083737
ISBN-13: 978-1461083733

Dedication

To my Mom and Dad
&
my Grandparents, Roy and Mae

Acknowledgements

When you sit down to write about the first 10 years of your life without the benefit of degree or experience you need someone to show genuine interest and offer an encouraging word. In that regard there are many people that I am grateful for: my husband, my kids, my brothers and sister, my nieces and nephews and first and foremost, my lifelong friend, Jo Alice. And to all those who listened attentively as I read my latest chapter, I thank you for your patience and kind comments. To Jo Alice and my son Blake who "sandpapered" my manuscript into existence, a special thank you. I could not have gotten it done without your help and expertise.

A few years back, when I started this project, my eight-year-old grandson asked if I was going to dedicate the book to him. While I will take the conventional path and dedicate my first writing attempt to my deserving parents and grandparents, I must admit, that as I wrote about my own childhood, my grandkids were very much on my mind. So, Mitch; to you and your brother and sister, and all your many cousins (first, second, and once-removed) I thank you for helping me remember how great it is to be a kid, especially if you have the good fortune, as I did, to have a family that loves you.

Contents

New roads; new ruts.

—Gilbert K. Chesterton

Chapter 1 — Dreams Denied

My first attempt at crisis intervention was focused on solving the problem of Mother's yelling. My younger brothers joined me in the northeast corner of the front room, where all three of us scrunched down between the arm of our worn-out maroon-colored couch and the front room wall.

Being the eldest, midway through my fourth year, I ruled my brothers pretty much as a benevolent dictator might preside over a third-world country. I had already learned by experience, that the threat of "telling Mom" was a powerful tool when trying to dictate to my siblings. Living with two little brothers had also convinced me that life went smoother when there was someone else to blame should events take a dangerous turn or start to move beyond my control.

As I began to lay out our strategy, Butch, at three years of age, was fully engaged but it was difficult to keep two-year-old Denny focused on the issue at hand.

"When she yells we'll just ignore her," I asserted. "O.K. guys?"

"Right," Butch volunteered enthusiastically.

Denny was busy picking at a small hole in the fading, fern patterned, gray linoleum.

"Right, Denny?" I demanded.

Denny raised his gaze from the floor and smiled, a signal I recognized as his support for a dangerous but necessary course of action.

It was not easy to ignore our Mother. She was a formidable presence on our Montana wheat ranch. She had been born in this house and raised under its roof while it was still referred to as a homestead. She had lived through dry, dusty summers, winter blizzards and the fickleness of grain and cattle prices.

Only as adults would her children eventually understand that Mom's yelling came from too much work, too many children, and a never-ending stream of hired men. And most of all, we would learn that this place we thought of as home was the last place on earth she wanted to be.

She was sure she had escaped the prairie when she married my Dad, an outsider, a fellow who had seen something of the world. Never mind that it had been from a boxcar as he and his brothers traveled the Hi-Line from St. Paul, Minnesota, to Seattle, Washington, looking for work during the depression.

As newlyweds, they had made it to the Pacific. It rained there. The streets were paved. Stores, theaters and hospitals were just around the corner. The grass was green. And there were trees and parks and best of all, the ocean. Mom's life was beginning to take shape just as she had always dreamed it would.

Ballard, just across the bridge from Seattle, was vibrant and booming during those early war years. Dad's brothers worked in the shipyards while Dad found a job with a young company called Boeing.

Their new home became a gathering place for the "boys" and their displaced North Dakota friends and acquaintances. The small apartment filled with young people, big band music blaring from the radio and constant speculation about what Roosevelt was going to do about Pearl Harbor. Smoke from their Camel cigarettes filtered through steamy diapers, often hung inside to avoid afternoon showers.

Undaunted, Mother pitched in with meals and advice for the homesick and war-worried young men. Loving the ocean and city life, she was immune from such anxieties. Her life was full of laughter and good times. Her tall, good looking husband had a steady job, she had a healthy little girl to care for and the Montana prairie was six hundred miles behind her. Life by the sea was full of promise.

As the brothers took turns bouncing their new niece from lap to lap, they discussed the ramifications of the draft versus volunteering. And then one day, without Mother's knowledge or approval, the four brothers went together to join up.

Mother was furious. Sending her husband off to war was not part of her plan. While it took a long time to get over being angry, she was relieved when Dad was classified "essential" because of his job at the aircraft factory. Health concerns caused Uncle Adolf to be classified "4F". Uncle Allen would soon be serving as a tail gunner based out of England and Uncle Bob would spend his time fighting from one Pacific island to the next.

As the war escalated and the streets of Ballard cleared of draft age young people, Mother filled her days with domestic chores and late afternoon walks with toddler and buggy up to the hills overlooking Puget Sound. Another baby was on the way and even a world war could not shake her confidence in the future. Her ties to the prairie were slipping away as serenely as the sun slipped behind the horizon far out over the Pacific.

Then Grandpa's letter arrived. He had shingles. He was in a bad way and hired help could not be found since every able-bodied man was off fighting a war. Could they come home and help out?

"Spring would be soon enough," he wrote. "Just so the seeding gets done in April. Your Mother and I wouldn't ask if we didn't have to."

And then he closed with a post script. "Please let us know as soon as you can."

As a country school teacher, Mom had travelled many rough and lonely Chouteau County roads. But here was the road she feared the most; the road back, retracing her steps, back to the ranch. How could she convince her young husband, who loved farming, that going home would only lead to a dead end? Hadn't they both agreed that the paved roads of Seattle had led them to the 'promised land'? She decided she would not go quietly.

Chapter 2 — Back to the Beginning

I have no memory of our move to Montana or any discussions that led up to that event. I didn't even notice that while Mom and Dad moved to Ballard with one child, they left with two, me and my new baby brother. I only knew that suddenly, like a ride on Aladdin's magic carpet, my home was on the prairie. The spaces around us were vast and wide open. The wind blew incessantly and the sky went on forever.

I do remember lots of green in Seattle. There had been high, green cupboards on the back porch where we lived. Green grass, green bushes and green trees surrounded my Mother and our friendly landlady as they visited in the back yard.

But now, back where she had started life, Mother was surrounded by brown. The fields, just turned over by the plow, were brown. The prairie grass, after waving green for just a few weeks each spring, turned brown. Even the air she breathed was dusty brown a good deal of the time. Instead of afternoon walks to the ocean, water had to be hauled from town to fill the cistern. It must have seemed to Mother that her dreams of a new life had dried up just like the caked, brown mud in the barnyard.

But one thing remained the same. The babies kept coming. Vaguely, I recall the day Dad gathered me in his arms and held me up to the radio as we listened to the Friday morning Baby News. Mom would soon be bringing home a second little brother.

In my new world, doting grandparents replaced boisterous uncles and an attentive landlady. Mother's parents lived twelve miles away in Fort Benton. Grandpa covered the dirt roads daily in his pickup truck to help out at the ranch. Grandma took care of the yard and house in town.

Their town property covered one quarter of a city block and was surrounded with huge, shady cottonwoods and clipped hedges. The property within was dominated by a large, comfortable home. Flowers, of every variety and color filled the yard and surrounded the red, concrete patio which ran from the front walk to the back door. Grandma even had furniture outdoors. There was a hammock for Grandpa's afternoon naps and a table and chairs where she served Kool-Aide and date stuffed sour cream cookies on hot summer afternoons.

The house was full of pretty things we were not allowed to touch. Newspapers crunched underfoot as they guided our dirty shoes from the back porch, across the dining room carpet into her spacious kitchen. Flowers, freshly picked, graced the dining room table and doilies adorned furniture we were not allowed to sit on.

At Grandma's house, we went to the bathroom indoors and took baths in a real tub upstairs. Baths at the ranch were weekly events, in a galvanized tub in the middle of the kitchen floor. With each young body, the water temperature would drop and the water gray. But Grandma's tub was equipped with hot running water and an orange plastic fish that circled the bather on currents of silky soap bubbles. Warm fluffy towels encircled us as Grandma lifted us from our bath. The word "luxury" was not yet in my vocabulary, but even a four year old ranch kid knows "really nice" when she experiences it first-hand.

Years of hard work had rewarded my grandparents with many good things and their beautiful home was constantly being improved or added on to. A large bedroom addition at ground level was topped by a deck that could only be reached from a door leading out of an upstairs bedroom. We thought of this door as an entrance way to heaven. Out on that deck, children of the treeless prairie mingled with leaves, branches and breezes that cooled our hot faces and shaded our suntanned skin. Drama and excitement were added on our roof top playground by playing close to the edge and with fake threats of pushing or jumping. We even considered swinging, Tarzan style, from overhanging branches but we knew that would result in Grandma kicking us off the roof and locking the door to heaven.

At the far south end of the lot was Grandpa's former butcher shop which had been converted into two small apartments. As Grandma administered this little piece of real estate we were often caught up in the drama of unpaid rent, disruptive visitors or sad partings when a favorite renter moved away.

This busy, beautiful place seemed like a fairy tale kingdom when compared to our drafty, isolated ranch house. No wonder we stood in line, hoping to be the lucky one invited to stay overnight with our grandparents.

My Grandma and Grandpa's home also served as a hub for family socializing. Nearly every Sunday we gathered at Grandma's house along with Aunt Dawn and Uncle Pierre and their daughter Vicky, who was born in between my two brothers. Pierre's parents, upon arriving from France, had homesteaded on the south side of the Missouri towards the Highwood Mountains.

My Uncle John, who had been adopted by my grandparents when he was about seven years old, sometimes joined us with his young family from Great Falls. He and Aunt Margaret had four children at that time, three of them older than us.

Aunt Doris, Uncle Fritz and Grandpa's namesake, Cousin Roy came from Spokane at least once a year, usually after harvest, for Grandpa's birthday.

Our Spokane cousin was a target for pranks and teasing. As an only child, Roy was used to being catered to and was unsuited, because of his asthma, for the rough and tumble activities of his ranch cousins.

"Now be nice," Mother would remind us on the ride to town. The burden of being "nice" fell mostly to my brothers since Roy was, after all, a boy and only a few months older than Butch. While visiting in town, Roy was relatively safe since his mother was always close at hand. It was when Grandpa brought him to the ranch that he was most at risk. If he tried being smarter or superior to his country cousins they would have him in tears before the day was over. If he went along with my brother's exploits the three of them usually ended up in serious trouble, like the time they tried to send smoke signals to Grandpa who was working the field south of the house.

"It's bad enough that you were playing with fire," Grandpa ranted when he arrived at the scene of their mischief. "But you built it right next to the gas tanks!"

8

Butch and Denny were quick to inform Grandpa that sending smoke signals had been all Roy's idea.

While uncles and cousins relaxed out on our grandparent's patio, Grandma would set two tables, one in the kitchen for the cousins and one in the dining room, with her good china, for the adults.

"Roy, get in here and eat," Grandma called impatiently as the food was carried to the table. For some reason she frequently seemed a little irritated with Grandpa.

"Yo!" he yelled back good naturedly as he came in from the patio followed by his grandchildren who had finally talked him into opening and sharing our birthday gifts to him. He had doled out just enough chocolate covered cherries and lemon drops to, according to Grandma, ruin our dinner.

After family dinners, while the women cleaned up and put the food away, the men wandered back out to the patio. Dad, if he got there first, would stretch out his long frame on the chaise lounge. Grandpa headed for his hammock while John, Pierre and Fritz pulled up patio chairs. The cousins played around and through the yard, carefully avoiding Grandma's flower beds, eventually spilling out onto the city sidewalk and around the block. It was the job of us older cousins to keep an eye on the younger kids and inform Grandma if anything was amiss, such as untrained country boys peeing in the alley.

As the afternoon progressed, Grandma would lead my apron clad Mother and Aunts on a tour of the yard. Each flower bed was visited and evaluated, ending with the roses, which led them directly back to the patio and their napping husbands.

Mildly interested in Grandma's growing things, I occasionally tagged along.

"What's that sweet smell?" I asked Grandma one afternoon, as we circled back towards the patio.

"That's Mock Orange" she told me. "It used to grow all over the hills when I was a girl back in the Idaho Territory."

"When I was a girl," signaled that we could ask her about the "old'en days". Cousins began to wander in from the sidewalk and gather around as she spun tales of wild horses, wolves, Indians and her parents coming from Arkansas in a covered wagon.

Later, as Grandma began to run out of stories and the men woke from their naps, leftovers were pulled out of the fridge and discussions turned to grain prices, religion, politics, or, my favorite topic; movies and movie stars.

As interesting as I found these conversations to be, they were usually cut short. There were cows to be milked back at the ranch.

Dad hated milking cows. He did it only because Grandma and Grandpa insisted on having milk cows and they were, after all, his boss.

"No matter what's going on," he complained, "I have to go home and milk those damn cows."

"Someday we'll have our own place and we won't have to milk cows," Mom would remind him.

"That's for damn sure!" he'd respond, pushing in on the clutch and shifting into third gear as we pulled up the hill out of Fort Benton.

Quarreling in the back seat finally ended as the battles for the window seats were settled, either by muscle or intimidation or by direct intervention from the front seat. As the last punch was thrown and the last wail ignored, we settled in for the ride home. Uphill and down, right turn or left, the moon followed us as Mom began to softly sing:

"Oh the moon shines tonight on pretty Red Wing,
The night winds sighing, the breezes crying,
As her brave lies dying, while Red Wings' crying
Her heart away."

Chapter 3 — Ranch Wife

Being a hard worker was what set one man apart from another in the days before men wore white collars to work. Keeping his fields clean of weeds, his livestock well cared for and his outbuildings in good repair were the marks of a good farmer. Being the first to get his seed in the ground each spring or hauling the first load of wheat to the elevator were the goals of every self-respecting, competitive rancher who was serious about providing for his large & growing family.

Ranch wives prided themselves on how well they fed the hired men or how many chickens they could butcher in a morning. Clean, well behaved children were another indicator that she was a productive and skilled ranch wife.

"He was a good worker," was Grandma's first response whenever I asked her about life with Grandpa. "No matter how tough times got, he was always able to make a few dollars to carry us through.

The neighbors, who were usually worse off than we were, knew your Grandpa could always find work. They depended on him for cash paying jobs when crops failed or babies got sick. Your Grandpa's contract with Great Northern Railroad pulled several Pleasant Valley homesteaders through some rough times," she told me.

Every summer, for a month or more, the neighbor men, each with a team of horses and a plow, joined Grandpa, turning the prairie over along one side of the railroad track all the way to Malta, and then, repeated the same process on the other side of the tracks back to Fort Benton. Meanwhile, their wives and kids stayed behind, taking on the extra chores that kept the homestead going for another season.

Correcting the standard version of history, Grandma reminded me that more farmers went broke during the twenties than did during the Great Depression.

"Plowing the fire guard for the railroad helped keep the bills paid during those grim dust bowl years. In the winter months, he cut ice on the Missouri River and sold it to the bars and restaurants in town. Then in the summer, he'd put up hay in the Shonkin Mountains. Anything to keep us going." Obviously proud of her husband, she declared, "he had a lot of gumption."

Visiting with her years later in the nursing home, I hoped that Grandma might go, for once, beyond the "hard worker" description of my Grandfather. I wanted to know something about his dreams and about their partnership as man and wife but for my Grandmother, life was not about romance, travel, hobbies or even "keeping busy". For her, life was about work and perseverance. In her opinion, a family without a good worker at its head was sure to fail and the grandchild who didn't learn the lesson of "never give up" just wasn't paying attention.

According to family lore, Grandma matched and sometimes exceeded her husband's work ethic. If the work was caught up at home and she could find someone to do the milking, she joined the fire guard crew as camp cook.

At harvest time, she worked in the fields alongside Grandpa and the hired men, as well as keeping them fed and her daughters cared for. Breaking for the mid-

14

day meal, Grandma would get the food on the table while the men lounged in the shade, like male lions waiting for a lioness to drag in a carcass for lunch.

Mom and Dad were also familiar with that sort of work ethic. They learned early, as teenagers during the depression that work was the only thing that guaranteed survival let alone getting ahead in life. Business hours extended beyond eight to five and there were no sick days or vacations unless you could squeeze in a few days in Glacier Park between harvest and seeding the winter wheat. Winters were welcomed as a chance to slow down, but there were still cattle to feed, roads to plow and machinery to be repaired.

Dad came from a hard working Norwegian immigrant family who settled in North Dakota in the 1880s. Dad's father lost his wife to a fast-talking neighbor and his farm to the bank during those same dust bowl days that so affected my Montana grandparents.

"They were good people," Dad told me when I was old enough to ask about his side of the family. "I don't know why my mother left. I was only seven at the time and I don't remember Dad never saying a word against her. For all I knew, I thought she'd be coming back."

Information about the break-up of their family was never imparted in one coherent chunk, but rather like eggs, laid randomly around the barnyard by chickens that had escaped the hen house. A tidbit here, a fact or theory there, but Dad and his seven siblings never approached the central tragedy of their lives without some trepidation. Aunt Florence, the oldest, probably ventured closest to the truth years later when we stopped to visit her in North Dakota.

"Do you know why Grandma left?" I cautiously inquired of my aging aunt, realizing that this might be my last chance to get a firsthand account of my Grandmother's one great sin.

I sensed Dad, who was traveling with me, stiffen. I was venturing into a world where I was not welcome, a world closed to outsiders.

Her eyes met Dad's as she considered, for a moment, difficult memories which I sensed were percolating to the surface like oil in a newly dug well.

"It was the work, I think. There was never any end to it. I remember one evening, walking out to meet her and Daddy as they came in from the fields. Mother was pregnant with the twins at the time and she looked so tired and drained I wanted to cry for her."

I pressed on. "But didn't you resent her for leaving you with all the work and the whole family to take care of?"

"Oh no, you couldn't be mad at Daddy or Mother. They were always so good to us. I think she just got tired and gave up."

Then she carefully and thoughtfully closed the door on the past. "Times were hard back then," she said, ending our conversation with the only explanation that must have made sense to her.

For Dad's part, he determined that his history would not dictate his future. He would work hard, keep his bills paid, get ahead, and his wife would not leave him behind with a handful of kids to raise.

Early on, he determined that the females in his household would not work in the fields. And even though Mother had a two year teaching degree, and there were times when cash crops were extremely scarce, she would not be teaching school. No matter how bleak their prospects, he would take care of her and those under his roof.

Even without field work, life was not easy for ranch wives. If you wanted fried chicken for dinner you had to catch, kill, clean and fry it. Pies were baked from scratch, vegetables brought in from the garden, milk separated in the cellar and butter churned. Clothes were hung on the line outside regardless of the temperature. Coal or wood was carried in to keep the kitchen stove ready for three hot meals a day.

With babies arriving nearly every year and, once the war ended, hired men to feed from spring to fall, Dad decided to hire someone to help mother whenever the need seemed most dire.

Most farm help was recruited from First Avenue South in Great Falls. There, men lined up outside a long strip of bars waiting to be hired by an overworked farmer or rancher. I learned about this place by observing from the back seat of our car as Dad scouted potential hires. If he found someone he thought could do the job, we would have to scoot together to make room for a stranger who had spent his last dollar on booze and was now in the process of sobering up.

These seedy, city streets were not the sort of place where you saw women or children so how Dad found Esther I'm not quite sure but he brought her home from Great Falls one evening, as proud and pleased with himself as if he was bringing Mother a dozen red roses.

"I know you are swamped with the hired men and all the cooking," he cooed to his exhausted wife. "Esther, here, can help you get on top of things."

Mother was appreciative. Harvest was fast approaching and the garden was coming on. She put Esther right to work getting supper on the table followed by clean-up while she got us kids off to bed.

But the next morning Esther did not feel well and arrived from the bunkhouse after breakfast was already on the table. There were apologies, of course, and understanding on Mother's part.

Over the next few weeks Mother attempted to get Esther on track. When she worked, even though occasionally cranky and confrontational, she did a good job. The trouble was that she could not be counted on to work consistently. Mother allowed that a person could be sick once in a while but she grew aggravated at Esther's frequent excuses and whining.

One day, Mother and Dad found it necessary to go back to Great Falls on business. Esther was left in charge with routine cleaning and meal preparation as her only assigned tasks. It was a beautiful summer day so Butch, Denny and I had very little reason to be inside except for the noon meal.

Coming in at lunch time, I noticed that Esther seemed unusually happy. She laughed a lot and for no apparent reason. Sensing a shift in Esther's personality, I came in often during the afternoon to check on Baby Jim. Peaceful and content, he seemed to be weathering Esther's mood change quite well. I, on the other hand, was becoming alarmed as her behavior seemed to grow more bizarre and unpredictable.

I was relieved when my parents finally arrived in time for a late supper which Esther was trying, at that very moment, to get under way.

I ran out to meet them as they got out of the car. "You better come quick," I urged. "Esther is acting really weird."

Mother was immediately distressed. "Did she do anything to you kids?"

"No, but she sure is acting strange."

Dad was concerned but cautious. "Now, Jean, don't get excited. I'm sure we can get everything straightened out. Just don't blow up and make her mad, you know what I mean?"

Hardly listening, Mother squared her shoulders and headed for her kitchen.

The smell of burned meat met us as we came through the screen door of the back porch. Entering the kitchen, we spotted Esther, propped up against the wall adjacent to the sink trying to peel potatoes.

"Oh, you're home," she announced to no one in particular. Her voice was slurred and much too loud. Giggling to herself, she went back to the potatoes, adjusting her stance against the wall so as to be more secure at the sink.

Mom and Dad stood transfixed, absorbing the chaos in the kitchen, the counters full of half-finished tasks and dirty lunch dishes. Smoke was wafting from the skillet on the stove. Denny's announcement that he was starving jolted them into action.

"She's drunk!" Mom snapped as she headed for the stove and the burning pork chops. Dad took over at the sink.

Taking charge, Mother began to bark out orders. "Butch, take Jimmy into the living room, Denny you go with him. Kareen you help Esther clean off that counter."

19

It was then that she noticed the cream sitting amongst the dirty dishes and cereal boxes on top of the kitchen counter.

"Has that cream been out all day?" she demanded of Esther. Esther wasn't sure.

The cream, after it was separated, was routinely stored in a gallon can on the top shelf of the fridge. Realizing that an inebriated Esther could probably not carry the cream and open the refrigerator at the same time, Mom ordered me to get the fridge door for her.

In spite of the tension spilling into every corner of the room, Esther seemed cooperative. With eyes fixed resolutely on the fridge, she staggered across the kitchen, gripping the cream can with both hands. And then, in slow motion, or so it seemed to me, I watched in horror as Esther flung the nearly full can of cream ceiling ward.

"Whee!" she yelled as slick, thick cream flew across the kitchen. It dripped from the ceiling and my hair. It spewed across the green linoleum. Even with the distraction of cream running down my shocked face I was pretty sure I knew what was coming next.

"Bill, get her out of here before I kill her!" Mom yelled.

Esther could hardly contain herself, giggling all the while, as Dad hustled her out the back door to the bunk house. As Mom and I struggled to corral the slippery cream we heard car doors slam and the car start.

"She's gone," Butch announced as he watched Dad turn the corner and head for town.

"Can we eat now?" was Denny's only concern.

Neighbor girls and cousins proved to be more reliable and pleasant helpers than the women Dad brought home from Great Falls. While younger (just kids, really) they could put in a full day's work as well as keep us kids entertained without the problems that down-on-their-luck women came equipped with.

We had teen-age cousins in St. Paul and several of them came west to help Mother during their summer breaks. Cousin Tom came first, a handsome teenager with lots of charm and a sweet nature. He was a city boy, uninitiated in the ways of ranch life, so he found everything exciting and interesting but often times, dangerous.

The same young man that braved traffic and bullies in St. Paul was fearful of snakes and horses. We found it unbelievable that he could be so panic-stricken at the rattle of a small snake or the crow hopping of a stubborn pony.

While a master at entertaining my brothers, who followed him as faithfully as Biblical disciples, Mother found Tommy too rambunctious to be of much help around the house.

One rainy day, I watched in dismay as Tommy and my brothers were using Mom and Dad's bed as a trampoline. Mother's mirrored dresser was at the foot of the bed, and one after another, they soared upwards, across the face of the mirror and back down again.

"You guys better stop that," I warned taking up my mantle of "boss" whenever Mom and Dad weren't around.

The gold and green velvety bed cover slipped and slid as stocking feet landed, again and again, on its surface. They were ignoring me.

I upped the ante. "You guys are going to get in trouble!"

21

Crash! The metal frame, the wooden slats, the mattress and the velvet bedspread all hit the floor with one mighty whack. Stunned and in shock, the three acrobats waded out of the bed covers just as Mom and Dad came through the back door.

"Bill, he's your nephew, do something with him," was all she said as she surveyed the rumpled mess, turned and retreated to the kitchen.

Tommy's sister, Donna, came the following summer.

I thought Donna was beautiful and as I watched adults interact with her, I think they thought so too. Her eyes were dark and thoughtful, her hair a shiny rich cocoa color but good looks were not her only attributes.

Street-wise, head-smart and organized, Donna came to us as sort of a super teenager. She and Tommy were the oldest in their family of nine and so she was used to kids and knew when and how to pitch in. Donna and Mother hit it off right from the start and remained lifelong friends. She fit so well into our family that there was talk, one summer, of her staying right through the school year.

She tried it, going off to school with the boys and myself for about a month but got too homesick or maybe just bored with our little country school.

Apparently, from what I could glean from grown-up conversations, young fellows in St. Paul were attracted to Donna and her sister Patti Ann like hippies to Woodstock. With black high heels, and slim, black sheath dresses, my city cousins were wired for excitement and fun. Mother suspected as much and dreaded the end of each summer when we put Donna back on the train to St. Paul. She was sure Donna would get herself into trouble and ruin her young life. "Promise me you'll behave yourself," she'd plead as she gave Donna one last hug before putting her on the east-bound train.

"I will, Aunt Jean. Don't worry." With hugs and kisses for her Uncle Bill and admiring cousins she boarded the train leaving us behind on the station platform. She was bound for good times in the big city and a life style that I could only imagine.

I pictured music and dancing, drinking and cigarettes, all in black and white, just like I'd seen in the movies. And truth be told, I was not too far off the mark.

But what she did in St Paul did not matter to any of us so long as we could count on her coming back to us the following summer which she did until we moved to town or she got in trouble. I can't remember which.

The summer I was six or seven, Dad hired our neighbor's daughter, Angie, to help Mom get through harvest. Since she was just entering her teenager years, I was impressed with everything she did and said. Watching her closely, I contemplated the sophistication and mystery of a thirteen year old. Someday, I told myself, I'll have bouncy wavy hair like Angie's. When I'm a teenager, I'll snap my gum just like Angie. Someday, but not too soon, I'll eat tomato sandwiches, just like Angie.

A few years later, after the car wreck that took Angie's life, I decided that being "just like Angie" was probably not a worthwhile goal. Angie had married only a couple of years after working for us and had two babies in quick succession She had died on impact when a car full of intoxicated teenagers left the highway one dark Saturday night. Her soldier husband came home, buried his wife, handed his babies over to Angie's parents and returned to duty.

I listened intently as the adults of the valley discussed the inevitability of a bad end for Angie. They concluded that she was too wild and fun-loving for her own good. It was hard for me to believe that Angie, perhaps one of the happiest people I had yet to meet in my young life, could bring such heartache to so many. But, nevertheless, I learned a lot from Angie.

I learned that a person can have too much fun. I learned that cars and fun don't necessarily go together. I learned that wives should be home with their babies and faithful to their husbands. And while, at the time, I did not understand what "wild" was all about, I learned to recognize its dangers whenever I ventured into similar activities during my own teenage years.

Unbeknownst to Angie, she had left me a legacy of caution and restraint. I would never be "just like Angie", a free and joyful spirit, but instead, a careful teen, tempering my need for fun with a desire to live and play another day.

Chapter 4 — Social Network

On the open prairie the definition of "neighbor" was expanded to include all those living within twenty miles of your home place. Whether it was helping to plow the roads after a blizzard or responding to unexplained black smoke, good neighbors were an essential part of ranch life. Their lives were very much like our own, revolving almost entirely around crops, livestock, the weather and the local schoolhouse. Whenever ranch work slowed down, "neighboring" picked up.

Oftentimes, if it had rained or the fieldwork was caught up, Dad would encourage Mom to invite someone down for cards.

"It'll be too wet to get in the fields in the morning, Jean. We might as well have someone over tonight."

Or the call might come first from one of our neighbors, inviting us to their house for cards or visiting. Regardless of where we ended up, I knew I would be overrun with small boys. The valley was infested with them. There wasn't another girl for miles in any direction.

The gender gap narrowed when we attended Friday night pinochle parties. Held at the schoolhouse after the fall fieldwork was done, the parties were family events. The Meeks family, with one daughter in tow, could be counted on to be present and so it would be Linda and me along with seven to ten younger boys playing out on a dark playground late into the night.

Light radiating from the schoolhouse windows and one lone yard light illuminated the playground but eventually we worked our games of tag or hide and seek farther out into the darkness.

There was only one rule. Every kid was aware of this iron clad regulation because their parents had lectured them on it, in the car, all the way from their home to the schoolhouse.

"Don't you dare, unless someone is bleeding, pester us while we're playing cards," our parents would order in the sternest voice possible.

Being the oldest and the only girls, Linda and I took it upon ourselves to be in charge out there in the dark. But, regardless of how hard we tried to maintain peace and order, there was always one crybaby in the crowd who ran bawling to his mother about something.

"They won't let me play," was a common complaint.

"Butch and Larry are picking on me," a younger boy might whine.

Or, "Kareen told me to shut up," was also heard occasionally.

If the night was young, these complaints usually brought an angry parent out on to the school steps, reminding us to behave ourselves and get along. If the night was late, the parent might play the last few hands with the distraught child on their lap.

Eventually we were called in to share a light supper with the grown-ups. Piling our plates with sandwiches, deviled eggs and cookies, we circulated among the crowd, admiring the prizes that had been awarded to the high point winners.

"Darn that John. He didn't let me have the bid all night," Mom might complain on the way home. "I bet he went set five times."

"Dot didn't have a clue what was going on," Dad might add if he and his partner had been on the losing end of the evening.

Knowing Dad liked to go home a winner, she'd tease back. "Well, at least you got the booby prize."

New blood was introduced to the farm community when a young farmer married a girl from town or from the other side of the Missouri River. If you were a farm girl you usually found yourself in your husband's neighborhood, perhaps a few miles north of Floweree or east of Loma.

But even in a new community, you were not a stranger because everyone in the county frequented Fort Benton for business and church and most of the young people went to Fort Benton High School.

My mother represented only the second generation of families in the tight knit community of Pleasant Valley. The bonds that had gotten the early homesteaders through drought, dust and the depression were still strong and secure and so my parents were welcomed back from Seattle as if they had never left.

It was unusual for a son-in-law to take over a farm, but for Grandpa it was inevitable since he was the father of three daughters and an adopted son who had no interest in farming. My grandparent's youngest, Aunt Dawn, had married a farmer who farmed with his parents in the south end of the county. Uncle Fritz, Aunt Doris' husband, was a sausage maker from Switzerland and knew nothing of farming. My parents, being his only remaining prospect, brought Grandpa to his desk to write that fateful letter that transported Mom, reluctantly, back to the 'home place'.

Mom knew nearly everything about everyone in Chouteau County and had strong opinions about who was decent and who was not. These opinions had been formed by her history. Sometimes her dislike could be traced to someone's cattle tearing out a fence and trampling out a grain crop or garden. Sometimes it related to those who had taken advantage of ranchers who were losing their land to the tax collector. She still remembered and reminded us about who did and did not pay their bills when, as a young girl, she delivered meat from Grandpa's town butcher shop. Her harshest criticism, however, was reserved for those she thought considered themselves better than other people.

"They think they're high mucky mucks," she'd remind anyone who dared fraternize with such types.

But she did appreciate and defend the underdog or the person trying, by honest means, to get ahead.

She knew and admired, for instance, our postman who had been wounded in the war but still found a way to maintain his livelihood as a rural mail carrier. Circling his station wagon in his wheelchair, he made the changes that allowed him to operate the vehicle with his hands rather than his feet. He also had the car mounted high up on special tires which would usually pull him through the gumbo that, with a good rain, turned dusty roads into something akin to wet cement.

Twice a week, rain or shine, like clockwork, Mr. Archer would deliver our mail to the corner mailboxes. As we watched him approach some miles to the south, we prepared to "rob the stage" just like we'd seen it done in the movies.

Quickly getting in costume, we strapped on our gun and holster sets, pulled on our cowboy boots, tightened bandanas around our necks and plopped on our cowboy hats. Running for the corner, we adjusted our red bandanas up over our faces. Sometimes, if we timed it just right, we met the mailman with guns drawn. If we got there before he did, we'd crouch down in the ditch readying ourselves for an ambush.

"Stick'em up," the three of us yelled in unison.

"Hand over that mail now!" Butch ordered with his six shooter aimed directly at the terrified mailman.

"Ya," Denny seconded, feet firmly planted and gun cocked.

The game fell flat if he had no mail for us that particular day.

"Sorry, guys, there's nothing for you today," Mr. Archer lamented, with shrugged shoulders and a friendly smile.

"Well, O.K. then," I sputtered in an effort to save face. "But you better have something for us next time or you're a goner!"

"I'll have something, don't you worry," and with a wave he plowed on to the next set of mailboxes, miles to the north.

Tom Rolf was another fellow Mother had a lot of respect for. Dad and Tom had become good friends when they both arrived from North Dakota at the same CCC camp in eastern Montana.

The Civilian Conservation Corps or CCC had been set up by the government to provide work during the depression for young men while at the same time assisting their families. The fellows in the program built roads, fences, irrigation dams, picnic grounds and the like. If need be, they even fought forest fires which Dad confessed to be one of the scariest things he had ever done in his life. The government provided room and board and paid the youthful workers thirty dollars a month. But they only got to keep five. A check for the remainder was sent to their struggling families back home.

After Tom's discharge from the army, he created a business that took him down nearly every lonesome road under the Montana sky. Maybe the quiet of the prairie and the meadowlark's song were healing forces after his wife took their baby son and moved to California. Whatever the motivation, Tom made his home in his van, traveling from ranch to ranch selling odds and ends that might be needed between the rancher's trips to town.

The back of the van was full of every imaginable notion and necessity—like a dime store on wheels. Needles and thread, scissors, razor blades, tape, small tools, nails, pencils and notebook paper, string, socks and underwear, hair ribbons and much more.

Whenever Tom was in Chouteau County, he was sure to stop by to visit with Dad. Knowing his family situation, Mom made a point of inviting him for supper and to spend the night.

Tom had his pride. "Well, only if you'll let me find something for you in the van," he insisted.

"Oh, I'm sure we can find something we need out there," Mom agreed with a wink in our direction.

While she got supper on the table, Dad and Tom ambled out to the van with us kids close on their heels. We were relegated to peering around them as Dad took his time checking out the tools.

"Got anything in here for kids?" Dad would eventually inquire when he thought we could stand the suspense no longer.

Tom joined in the torture. "Maybe we could find a few things kids like. But I don't know. I'm kind of short on merchandise this trip."

They rummaged a while longer.

Hovering over the back door of the van, backsides to us, they would continue the game. "No, I don't think kids would like that," Tom might offer. "But how about this?"

"Maybe some kids, but not mine." Dad showed no mercy.

"Let us see!" we begged, jumping up and down and sideways trying to see inside Mr. Rolf's treasure trove.

Finally, they'd back away and let us scramble to the front. Tom knew how to spot the gleam in a kid's eye and watched us carefully as we examined the merchandise. We were not allowed to touch but if he saw our eyes lock on to something he'd hand it to us.

"You like that?" he'd ask. If we shook our heads yes, it was ours. Sometimes it was a pin-wheel or a ruler, or a balsa wood airplane kit or a whistle. My brothers especially liked the click pens.

After each of his kids had a gift in hand, Dad would buy something he needed and a few dollars would change hands. And of course, there would be a new pot holder for mother or maybe a bar of sweet smelling soap.

As far as Mother was concerned, most of our hired men also deserved our respect. Some of them were drunks and thieves but most of them were men who were down on their luck or who had experienced some

31

rough breaks in life.   And our Dad, who had been forced by dire circumstances, to live the life of a hired hand, was always ready to give them a break.

"I know how it feels to have cars pass you up when you're hot and tired," he'd explain whenever he'd stop to pick up a hitchhiker, which he did on almost every trip to or from Great Falls.

"Move over back there," he'd order pulling the car on to the shoulder of the highway. As the stranger ran towards our waiting vehicle, we held a quick family meeting.

"I don't know, he looks a little spooky to me," Mom would advise.

"We don't have room for him," might be the conclusion of the back seat crowd.

"You can make room." Dad always had the final vote.

Hitchhiker protocol required the stranger to pause at the door and wait for an invitation to get in the car.

"Where you headed?" was my father's standard question.

The answer might be specific. "Got a job waiting for me in Havre," or it might be vague, "as far as you'll take me."

"Get in," was always Dad's response.

While we adjusted bodies and bags in the back seat, Dad locked eyes with our new passenger through the rearview mirror, exchanging pleasantries.

"Sure do appreciate the ride, Mister," and with a nod in mother's direction, "Ma'am."

"Where you from?" was question number two. That answer was often vague as well but, sometimes, there was a long, sad story that unraveled as we traveled, cramped and confined, down the highway.

As we approached our turn off to the ranch, Dad slowed the car and pulled over to the side of the road. "This is as far as we go. Good luck to you."

With a wave and the stranger's thanks we pulled away, down the gravel road towards home. Evaluating the experience came next.

"Whew, he smelled like a brewery," or "we're lucky he didn't murder us all," were occasional comments, but usually, we were touched by the hitchhiker's good manners and soft speech. As we watched him disappear behind us, just a speck now on the vast open road, we found ourselves wishing him good fortune and hoping he wouldn't have to wait too long before he caught another ride to cover that last seventy miles to Havre.

Our red, square bunkhouse stood in the center of the ranch buildings just a few yards from the house. The rule, always enforced and absolutely unbreakable, was that kids did not go in the bunkhouse. Over the years our bunkhouse served as a temporary home for many men and a few women who arrived and departed as the work demanded. Some were surly and quiet, some tough and impatient, but most seemed happy to fit into family life even if it was only for a season.

Clark, a young man looking for adventure out west, had hitchhiked all the way from Wisconsin to Fort Benton, where Dad found and hired him to help with spring seeding. He proved to be such a good worker and so pleasant that he stayed through fall work and came back several summers thereafter.

My memories of him are especially fond since he was the one who finally taught me how to keep my bicycle upright. After a long hard day in the field, and quite a little bit of begging on my part, Clark would help me push my new bike up the road east of the house. Once at the crest of the hill he held me and the bike steady while I attempted to get my balance. Then with one big push, he sent me down the slope, back towards the ranch house. The speed was thrilling and the crashes spectacular, until at last, one warm summer evening, I applied the brakes at the bottom of the hill, set my right foot down in the dust and turned to smile back up at Clark. He and my brothers were cheering wildly, celebrating my accomplishment. For the very first time, at six years of age, I fell in love.

Another of our favorite hired men was Ed. He was lean and hard and older than most of Dad's workers. Ed was a master at building kites. On quiet Sunday afternoons he put sticks, brown paper and binder twine together, forming kites bigger than our kitchen table. Then all he had to do was wait for the wind, which never seemed to take too long.

As the wind ripped, the huge kite soared for what seemed like a mile into the big, blustery Montana sky. Ed would let us take turns flying his kite. It was thrilling to feel the power of the wind as we were pulled overland like water skiers behind a ski boat.

Ed taught us how to plant our feet firmly and lean back with all our might. I worried though when Ed handed the kite off to Denny. Too small to brace himself, I watched in dismay, as Denny ran, stumbled and finally fell, still holding on to the straining binding twine with his stubborn little hands. The kite was pulling him face down, over and through the dirt clods in the field.

"Let go! Let go!" I yelled, but Denny was determined to hold on.

Scrambling, Ed and Butch raced to catch up with Denny before the kite was jerked away or Denny and the kite disappeared over the shelter belt. Spitting mud from his mouth and rubbing dirt from his eyes, Denny begged Ed to let him try again.

One warm fall day I was busy rummaging in the junk pile on the shady side of the shop. Dad and his latest hired man, George, were working inside, fixing something or other. At some point their conversation took an interesting turn. My ears perked up.

With some urgency in his voice, George was telling Dad that he would be leaving the next day.

Dad urged him to reconsider. "There's work here till the snow flies. Why not stick around till then?"

"Can't do that," George replied emphatically.

Dad pressed him. "Why not? What's your rush?"

I could sense the seriousness and intensity of what followed right through the shop walls. Always eager to know everything that was going on, I settled myself on an old bucket, close to the shop door, so as not to miss a single word of this adult interchange.

Somberly, George continued. "I've been here longer than I should have been already, Bill. You see, there's a warrant out for my arrest and I just feel like it's time to move on before they catch up with me."

"A warrant? For what?" Dad sounded as though he was having a hard time believing that this quiet, gentle man could be a law breaker.

George's voice dropped an octave. I strained to hear.

"Murder," I heard him mumble.

Murder! I almost fell off the bucket! Choking back a violent gasp, my mind raced. What was Mom going to say? What was Dad going to do?

Dad was incredulous. The only questions left to ask were who and how.

"It was an accident," George explained quietly, "but no one believed me. When I heard they were coming after me, I just lost it and took off. I've been on the run for nearly three years now."

I slipped away from the junk pile and headed for the shelter belt. I needed some quiet time to think about what I had just heard.

I'd never known a murderer before; at least that I knew about. And that was the crux of the problem. I couldn't count on what I thought I knew about people anymore. Never, in a million years would I have suspected that George had killed someone. He was polite to Mother, considerate of Grandpa and Dad, hard working, and fun and playful with us kids. Everyone liked him and I knew that Dad considered him to be one of the best hired men we'd ever had.

We said our goodbyes the next morning after breakfast. Dad counted out some bills on the table, added a small bonus and shook George's hand. With tears welling up in her eyes, Mother gave him a hug and a pat on the back.

Like small men, Butch, Denny and even Jimmy lined up to shake his hand which culminated in a four way bear hug. At last George turned in my direction.

I had been considering my family's fond farewell to this confessed killer. Were they all being duped by false charm or was George really just a good man in a bad spot? I decided, then and there, that I could only rely on what I knew for certain, and I knew, without a doubt, that George had proved to be a warm and trusted friend and that I would miss him.

I fell into his waiting arms and hugged him with all the sincerity I could muster.

"Goodbye, old girl," he smiled. "You keep an eye on those brothers of yours and don't let them do anything I wouldn't do!"

Chapter 5 — *Thoroughly Modern*

My grandparent's tired old farmhouse had not been occupied for many years. After they moved to town so their girls could attend high school, the place pretty much fended for itself, absorbing the blizzards, the wind and the dust, alone, without much human intervention.

All that changed when we moved into the house. It seemed as though something was in a constant state of being fixed, replaced or added on to. Making the house more comfortable and Mother's workload lighter, Grandpa and Dad were continually investing time and money into home improvement projects.

In the beginning, there was a sort of carbide gas lighting system which protruded from the walls of each room and required a match to ignite. Mounted high up on the wall, near the ceiling, it was left to the adults to light and extinguish the fixture. The last thing I remember as Mother tucked us in each night was the afterglow, as she reached up and turned off the gas lamp.

There was also a huge coal burning cook stove in the northeast corner of the kitchen, with a coal box nearby. Knowing when to add coal to the stove and how much, determined the quality of the cakes, roasts and pies that would eventually come out of the black oven.

The top of the stove was flat and wide, an ideal place to cook lefsa, which my grandmother and aunts on Dad's side of the family did whenever they came for visits. There was also a deep cavity near the stove fire box that was always kept full of water for dishwashing or an occasional cup of tea.

Recessed lids were built into the top of this wide surface and were lifted out with handles, revealing the red hot coals below. These lids made it easy to get rid of unwanted paper and trash. In fact, the stove welcomed and put to good use all the junk we stuffed into the fire box. We kids thought it was great fun to watch the flames dance upward, consuming whatever offerings an adult might bring to it, until one night the fun turned into a horror show directed by my teasing father.

"I'm going to eat it, Kareen! I'm going to cook it and eat it!"

Blood drizzling from the dead mouse, sizzled as it fell into the flames below. The fire snapped and roared, greedily reaching with fiery fingers for the mouse suspended from my Dad's glowing finger tips. His eyes flashed as his handsome face was transformed into a red evil that one might expect to encounter only at the gates of hell.

Screaming, I covered my ears and closed my eyes to the horror of mouse blood dancing on the hot surface of the stove.

"Stop, stop!" I begged, hiding my face in Mother's apron.

"Bill, for God's sake! Stop tormenting her. You know she's scared to death of mice," Mother ordered as she tried to make herself heard over my ear-splitting screams.

With one last wicked laugh, Dad let the mouse drop into the burning pit and replaced the stove lid. The kitchen darkened a bit as the fire retreated into its black hole. Sensing the end of the ordeal, I slowly opened one eye and then the other.

"That was mean!" I snapped as my Dad squatted down beside me.

"I'm sorry, Honey, but it was just a little dead mouse. What are you so afraid of?" he asked, trying to make amends.

"I don't know," I cried into his shoulder. "It was just so scary! And you were scary too," I wailed.

Dad spent the rest of the evening dishing out extra assurances, promising to never again tease me with a mouse. This promise probably required some discipline on his part since he was a chronic tease and our old farmhouse always had a rodent or two.

Shortly after we moved to Pleasant Valley there was talk about electricity coming through to the farms in the area. I had no idea what electricity was but I knew what it did. I knew it turned on the lights, baked the biscuits and heated the water at Grandma's house in town.

Mom yearned for a new electric stove. An electric stove would eliminate the task of carrying black, dirty coal into the house every day. Her kitchen would be cleaner and her cakes moister.

Dad and Grandpa bided their time as the workmen strung power lines through the valley and past our place. While they waited, they busied themselves planting poles strategically around the farm, with one each at the barn, the shop and the house. Lines were then strung overhead, between the poles. Farm work slowed as wiring the house became their top priority. And then one day, they flipped a switch and the lights came on. The bulky, black coal stove was wrestled out the back door just as Mother placed a celebration cake in her new electric oven.

Electricity changed our lives. Now, we kids were nagged to turn off the lights when we left a room. During bad weather we parked ourselves, for hours, in front of the new, console radio/record player listening to the adventures of *'Uncle Remus'*, *'Bozo the Clown'* or my favorite, *'So Dear to My Heart'*. And with electricity, games could continue long after the supper hour, played under the glow of our new yard light.

Another home improvement project was tearing off the old screened porch and replacing it with a new living room. I hated to see this happen because it meant removing the only real tree on our place. I had to admit, though, that it wasn't good for much. Somehow, in its struggle to survive, its roots had gone looking for water underneath the porch, pushing up the porch floor in the process. Consequently, the tree didn't stand up straight but leaned precariously out over the front yard. That created a great place for kids to climb but a poor provider of shade and respite from the summer sun.

It didn't take long for the tree to come down and the porch to be ripped off. Then there were workmen all around, sawing and pounding as they helped Dad and Grandpa build Mother's new room.

"Stay away from the front of the house when we're out there working," Dad warned, convinced that one of us was sure to get maimed or injured.

But the hammers and saws were irresistible to the boys and, for my part; I just needed to know what was going on. Gradually we worked our way on to the building site.

If Grandpa was out of nails, Butch volunteered to go to the shop for more. If one of the carpenters was thirsty, Denny brought him a glass of water. It didn't take long before we were all underfoot from the first nail pounded in the morning until they put their tools away each afternoon.

"Watch those old boards," we'd be warned. "They're full of rusty nails." Eventually, just as Dad had expected, there were casualties.

Jimmy, who followed his big brothers everywhere, was the first victim. As he climbed up and over the old boards he found one of those nails, driving it through his shoe, into his foot. He spent the rest of the project inside with Mother.

When the next accident came, it was not from below, but from overhead. A workman, somehow, dropped his hammer directly on Butch's head. There was a lot of crying and blood, followed by a trip to town for stitches. For Dad, this was the last straw. From that day on the men finished the project without our help.

It turned out to be a fine room with a front door and a long bank of windows. Mother got a new couch that attracted the attention of us all. Proudly demonstrating the couch's features, Mother lifted the front of the seat, pulled it towards her and then nudged it back towards the wall. We heard a clicking sound and then, right before our eyes, the couch turned into a bed.

"And there's room underneath to store blankets and pillows," she boasted. "Now we have someplace for company to sleep and room to entertain." She was proud of the new addition, the one place she could keep free of clutter and ready for visitors at a moment's notice. In the years to follow our Christmas tree was erected in the corner of the room, but mostly, the space was off limits to the family.

With the arrival of electricity, Grandpa implemented a plan that he had been contemplating for some time. Water for the house had to be hauled from town and flushed into a cistern, and from there, into the house, where a hand pump brought it up a pipe and into the kitchen.

The well at the reservoir was the only known source of water for miles around and it just happened to be in the middle of my grandparent's small pasture across the road from the house. When the reservoir dried up, water for thirsty cows and horses was brought to the surface by a windmill. When there wasn't enough wind to turn the windmill, someone had to go up to the well house and pump the water to the surface by hand.

With electric power, bringing water from the well directly into the house, was now, Grandpa thought, a possibility. Since the house was lower than the well, he planned to use gravity flow to bring water down to the yard and house. The wind or lack of it would no longer be a factor since electrical pumps would guarantee a reliable, consistent flow. It wasn't long before the stock tanks at the reservoir and the corral were full and Mother had running water, with a turn of the faucet, in the kitchen.

Grandpa's technological advancements did not extend to an indoor bathroom. Maybe he was working on ideas for how to add a tub and toilet, I can't say for sure. But I do know that, in spite of all the improvements to the old ranch house, we continued to travel to and fro on the wooden walkway to the outhouse.

Some lifestyle changes, which seem minor, now, were huge at the time. The introduction of a cheap, tasty, replacement for butter brought an end to churning our own spread. Churning butter was a job kids could do and so Butch, Denny and I were assigned churning chores each Friday.

Churning started out easy and got more difficult as the cream became thicker and turned to butter. Getting to the butter stage took a considerable amount of time and churning was, after all, a chore. And chores were something we tried to avoid or at the very least, finish quickly so we could get back outside.

"I think it's done," we'd announce with every tenth turn of the crank.

"Just keep going," Mom would order without so much as a glance in our direction.

Leaning into the crank with grunts and groans did not fool her.

"Another ten minutes should do it," she'd announce without even checking inside the churn.

Finally, when we thought we could not get those paddles around one more time, she would take a peek.

"Almost there. Just a little bit longer." Now our groans were for real.

By contrast, squeezing the margarine bag was a chore we didn't object to. Whenever Mother brought margarine home in her grocery bag, we would fight over whose turn it was to squeeze the yellow food coloring tablet into the white, plastic encased butter substitute. This process didn't take forever like churning did and we considered it much more satisfying and creative as we manipulated the yellow dye through the package.

The most profound change in our living standard; even bigger than electricity, was the addition of a telephone on our kitchen wall. This marvelous invention came with some warnings, however.

"Never go near the phone if there's a lightning storm," Dad cautioned as he connected the wires coming into the house to the wires in the wooden telephone box. "Lightning will travel right through the wires and into the telephone. If you're on the phone at the time, it'll kill you deader than a doornail. "

I didn't think it would really "kill" us. I thought Dad was probably just exaggerating to scare us. But I learned otherwise, one wild July day, when a fierce and dangerous thunderstorm roared across the valley

We kids had gathered, together with Mom, in the kitchen to watch the storm from the safety of four walls and a sturdy roof. The wind was on a tear, the rain was very close to the hail stage and the thunder and lightning were booming and flashing all around us Butch and Denny were observing all this from the kitchen window, the window next to the phone.

With a terrifying boom, thunder shook the windows and rattled the dishes I was setting out on the table for the supper meal.

Mother only had a fraction of a second to scream for the boys to get away from the window, when with a crack like a swift and powerful slap to the face, an electrical jolt charged through the phone, past the kitchen table, through Mom and Dad's open bedroom door and out their window on the other side of the house.

It only took a few seconds more for Butch and Denny to pick themselves up off the floor and run screaming into Mother's skirt.

I, for once, was dumbstruck, unable to move. My one and only thought was that I should probably take Dad's warnings more seriously in the future.

I didn't take Mother too seriously, either, when she warned us to be careful about what we said over the phone. "And Bill, no cuss words!" she admonished.

"Why not?" I asked.

She was impatient with my penchant for always questioning the obvious.

"Because the operator will report you to the phone company and they will come and take our phone away, that's why!"

I was sure there was a flaw in her reasoning somewhere. "But you said that it was wrong to listen in on other people's phone calls. How will the operator know that Dad is cussing if they can't listen in?"

"Oh, they'll know," she insisted. "Those operators are going to know everything that's going on in the whole county, believe you me. So, if I were you, I'd watch what I say." Mother guarded all personal information as though she had direct ties to the CIA.

But kids didn't use the telephone unless they were invited to by an adult. First, someone had to want to talk to you. Next, a chair had to be dragged over to the phone so you could reach the receiver and then, since it was a party line, you had to say what you were going to say and get off the line. All of this considered, it seemed to me, highly unlikely that my conversations would cause the telephone company to come for our phone.

As our neighbors were added to the phone line we began to memorize their individual rings. Cranking the handle on the right side of the phone box, according to which phone you wanted to reach, would cause every other phone on that line to jingle. To call someone in town required one long, insistent turn of the crank. "Hello, Central? Hello?" the caller would shout into the phone, "61-J please."

Our ring at the ranch was two longs and five shorts. As the calls went out amongst the neighbors, we knew who was being called by the ring patterns. And Mom and Dad got very good at identifying voices since the only way to know when the line was free was to pick up the receiver and listen for a second or two. If people were talking, you were supposed to hang up, avoiding the temptation to listen. If no one was on the line, you went ahead and called through.

"They're talking to Ida," Mom informed Dad as he tried repeatedly to use the telephone one morning. "She's been on the phone for over an hour. Just bang on the hook a few times and maybe they'll get the message and hang up."

"I've already tried that twice," Dad complained. "I need to order those parts before noon so your Dad can bring them out."

"Then just butt in and tell them you have to use the phone," Mom advised.

In a crisis or an emergency, or with Ida, this was acceptable telephone etiquette.

And one day, it saved three lives.

Mother got Ida's unwelcome phone call on a cold winter morning. With many chores still to accomplish, she was trying to get off the line while Ida droned on and on about some insignificant planning detail for the upcoming card party.

Suddenly, Mother was jolted to attention by a voice she thought she recognized.

"Help us. Please, somebody, help us," the voice pleaded.

"Ida, did you hear that?"

Ida, immediately alert and focused for a change, shot back, "It sounded like Irene!"

"I'm sure of it. Something's wrong up there!" Mother shouted into the telephone. "You call the neighbors. Bill and I'll head up there right now."

"What do you think is going on?" Ida asked, reverting to her tendency to discuss everything in detail.

Mother, always a woman of action, was already grabbing her coat from the rack beside the telephone. "We're going now, Ida. Call everyone you can and get them up to the Cox place."

The receiver was barely back on its hook, when she shouted at me to watch my brothers and stay off the phone. Yelling for Dad, out in the shop, she hit the yard running. A feeling of dread gripped me as I watched them jump into the car and head east at breakneck speed.

With my nerves on edge, I jumped as the phone began jangling. Ida's cranking had urgency to it as each call was quickly followed by another. Three longs and then one short was Meeks' ring. Two longs followed by two shorts was the Eloffs', and so it went until the ringing of the telephone was replaced by cars

49

and pickups flying past our house, all headed for the Cox place.

Isolated and uninformed I imagined the worst, terrified at what my parents and our neighbors might be dealing with. Then just as suddenly as they came, cars began speeding by in the opposite direction, ours among them. At the corner, they turned towards town.

Tom and Kate's vehicle, at the end of the line, slowed and turned into our yard.

"Your folks are taking Elmer, Irene and the baby to the hospital," they informed me as I met them at the door. "They want you kids to come up to our place until they get back."

While Kate helped me bundle Jimmy into his snowsuit she and Tom filled me in on what had happened.

"Well, we don't know the whole story," they began. "Everything was happening so fast by the time we got there. Apparently, Irene and Elmer were unconscious when your folks arrived. They'd been varnishing their floors and somehow were overcome by the fumes. All three of them were outside in the snow when we got there and your Mom and Dad were trying to get them awake. Elmer still hasn't come to, but we're pretty sure Leon and Irene will be O.K."

We arrived at Eloffs' just as their telephone began to ring. It was Dad.

"We got Elmer awake about halfway to town," he reported. "I think all three of them are going to be fine. The doctor is checking them over right now, but my guess is they'll be spending a few days in the hospital. Tell the kids we'll be home in a couple of hours."

With that, the crisis was over. It was only later we learned that the strong smell of varnish had disguised gas fumes leaking from a faulty heating system. Elmer and Irene didn't realize the danger until it was almost too late.

"When Leon fell asleep in his playpen I thought he was just taking an early nap but when Elmer passed out I knew something was terribly wrong," Irene related after returning from the hospital. "I knew my only hope was the telephone but it took all I had to get to it."

When Mom and Dad arrived on the scene, they realized they had to get the house open and do it quick. Mother threw open the doors and smashed windows as Dad struggled to pull Elmer and Irene outside. Mother grabbed Leon and rushed him out into the cold winter air, probably saving him from brain damage or worse.

As the neighbors arrived they helped load Elmer and his family into waiting vehicles. With Mom driving, Dad climbed into the back seat with Elmer. Slapping, yelling and shaking him, Dad finally was able to rouse him just as Mom cruised down Chinaman Hill going as fast as she dared on icy, gravel roads. "He's coming around!" Dad yelled from behind her.

"Thank God!" Mom responded as she led the speeding vehicles to the back door of the hospital.

Ida, again attending to details, had the foresight to call ahead to the hospital. Doctor Anderson and several nuns met the cars as they pulled into the hospital driveway. Quickly they helped unload the disoriented family and move them inside.

Who or what was responsible for saving three lives that cold winter day was rehashed by the neighbors many times that winter. Was it Irene who managed to get to the telephone or was it the quick action of their neighbors? Or maybe it was the doctor and his team? A unanimous conclusion was not hard to arrive at.

"Without the telephone, we'd have been goners." Elmer confessed.

Mother offered with a laugh, a twist to his logic. "Well, I think you should thank your lucky stars that Ida called me that morning and I couldn't think of a polite way to say "goodbye."

Chapter 6 – Skates, Scooters & Concrete

For ranch kids nothing improves your standard of living like a night in town with the grandparents. At Grandma's house the toilet was indoors, the water was hot, the yard shady and, best of all, the entire neighborhood was full of kids.

As we became acquainted with our peers we were surprised to learn that the town kids were terrified of our Grandmother.

"She's your grandma?" they would ask in shocked disbelief.

"Ya, so what?" we'd counter to their rolling eyes and expressions of mock horror. None of them could believe that we really liked our family's matriarch.

The sentiment of the neighborhood kids was unanimous. "She's the meanest old woman in the whole world!"

"Cripe, if you even touch her precious grass she yells at you," a heavyset girl about my age informed us angrily.

"Ya, and she glares at us every time we ride our bikes on her sidewalk," one of the older boys volunteered.

We knew our Grandmother was strict. If you looked at her fashion magazines you had to stack them back under the library table exactly the way you had found them. If she caught you cutting across the grass instead of following the right angle of the sidewalk you were sent back to the front walk and ordered to come in the "right way." If you went to the store for her you had to account for the exact change and if you, per chance, got the wrong item she would send you back to the store to correct your mistake.

We knew we couldn't come in the front door, that we couldn't sit on her brocade chairs in the parlor and that you never, ever picked a flower in her yard without her permission.

Life at Grandma's house was all about following the rules. Stay straight and the town was yours. Screw up and you were in the next pickup leaving town. Her demands were clear, concise and consistent.

Adherence to the rules kept discipline to a minimum and allowed Grandma to enjoy our visits. Keeping us entertained was not difficult since there were so many things to do that were impossible on the farm.

At first there was roller skating on the sidewalk beyond the hedges. Each grandchild had their own skates which hung on nails in the stairway to our grandparent's basement.

Time and patience were required to keep Butch, Denny and myself on our feet and rolling forward. First, we had to match our shoes to the skates, adjusting the length and breadth of them as needed. Next, we tightened the front skate brackets around the toe of our shoes until the rubber soles crunched up like raw bread dough. Then we pulled the leather strap up around our ankle and tightened it in the furthest hole possible.

Now we were ready to stand on our own two skates. But that was no easy task as Grandma worked to steady and maneuver us around the patio furniture and out to the city sidewalk.

"Now, whatever you do, don't lose your skate key," she'd warn as she slipped the string and key around our necks and, with a nudge, sent us out on the cracked concrete to fend for ourselves.

Of course there were wrecks, skinned knees, scraped palms and lots of tears. We knew that long, loud wails would bring Grandma running. Serious wounds earned us a gentle dose of first aide and a tall glass of Kool-aide. Superficial injuries would be dismissed as she picked us up and encouraged us to keep trying.

More often than not, one of us would soon be hop scotching back to the patio with one skate on and the other dangling from our ankle where the entire process would begin all over again.

Skating turned out to be a lot of work for Grandma. Maybe that's why, one fine day, Butch, Denny and I found three red scooters waiting for us on the patio. We didn't know what to do with them at first but the adults quickly convinced us that scooters were the only way to go.

No adjustments for shoe size were required. And there were no buckles or brackets breaking loose just as you reached the far side of a bulge in the sidewalk. Scooter technology was easy to master; push with your free foot, then coast as far as your forward thrust would take you.

Within minutes, with our right legs churning, we were pushing confidently around the block on our sporty new scooters, the envy, we thought, of every kid we passed.

Meanwhile, back at the patio, Grandma was enjoying a cold glass of ice tea, the company of her adult daughters and feeling very clever indeed.

Eventually, as each grandchild turned six years of age, they graduated from scooters and skates to a shiny new bicycle, a birthday gift from Grandma and Grandpa.

Mine was true blue with silver trim and a basket on the front of the handle bars. Butch and Denny simmered with envy as Grandpa walked the two-wheeled masterpiece out from the garage on to the patio.

"Holy cow!" I exclaimed in disbelief. "It's really mine?" It was hard to believe that just turning six could yield such rewards. But there was probably a catch and I decided to find out what it was right from the start.

"Do I have to share it with the boys?" I asked, bracing myself for the let down that I was sure was coming.

"Not unless you want to," Grandpa responded, with a wink in the boy's direction.

Inwardly I smiled an evil smile. "Not in a million years," I silently promised myself.

The afternoon was spent balancing me on the seat of my new bike as the grown-ups took turns running alongside, back and forth, on the sidewalk in front of Grandma's house.

Dejected, Butch and Denny stood on the sideline taking in the spectacle, as one after another of the exhausted adults dropped out of the activity. The boys knew me well enough to know that I was not going to be able to master that bike any time soon.

"Let me try! Let me try!" they began to shout as the afternoon wore on and the adults began to express doubts about my balance and coordination capabilities.

"You guys just shut up!" I shouted back over my shoulder as Grandpa, in a slow jog, struggled beside me, trying to keep me and the bike upright.

One moment of distraction was all it took. Before I could turn my eyes forward, I had run off the sidewalk, fallen off the bike and knocked my Grandfather into the hedge.

Grandpa came up out of the hedge in a huff. "Young lady, that's no way to speak to your brothers. Now if you don't want to pay attention and be nice, we can just put this bike back in the garage for a few days," he threatened.

The running and pushing came to a close with about four more trips up and down the sidewalk. Denny and Butch remained silent as ordered while I tried, without success, to keep the bicycle balanced as its rolling wheels outdistanced my worn-out supporters.

Every trip to town was now dedicated to learning how to ride my bike. As the adults began to avoid my pleas for help, I had to resort to bribing my brothers. I hated to let them near my bike but without them, I was pretty much left to figure out the laws of gravity all by myself. So I offered them a deal.

If they would help me I would let them have a turn. Now all three of us were crashing onto the sidewalk and falling into the hedge. My beautiful blue bike was taking a beating.

Dad finally came up with a suggestion that turned the tide. "Maybe if we took the bike to the ranch she could try coasting down the hills and get her balance better."

"At least the dirt would make for a softer landing," Mom joked.

"And we wouldn't have to do so much running," Grandpa laughed.

From an early age, Grandma herded her grandchildren to the library, which was only three blocks from her house. The boys were not impressed with the Carnegie building and its contents and eventually they dropped out of the activity.

"All the better," I thought to myself. "They can't keep quiet in there anyway."

Visiting the public library was an education in more than just books. Borrowing and returning them was my first introduction to the world of 'being responsible'.

"Don't forget your library books are due the end of the week," Grandma would remind me politely.

"You're going to have to pay your own fine this time," she'd threaten weeks later as she helped me shake out the covers, scrounge under my bed and dig through the toy box for a missing volume.

"Kareen, the library called again. Have you found that book yet?" Her effort to instill in me, a responsible and organized approach to life was driving her to distraction.

Eventually the lost book would turn up, weeks or months later, in some unexplained location, like the bottom of a doll buggy. Grandma would pay the fine, which obligated me to do odd jobs until the money was paid back. Occasionally, she would have to pay for a book that was never found. Finally, realizing that the head librarian was made of sterner stuff than she, I was cut loose and made to deal directly with a government bureaucracy. The librarian's continual threat of canceling my library card hovered over my head like a wind-whipped, rain soaked umbrella.

Grandma loved to read. She preferred westerns and crime stories to all other types of literature. I, on the other hand, liked biographies and was captivated by the long rack of orange books in the children's section, each containing the life story of some famous person. I vowed to read them all and was closing in on my goal when I hit the biographies of baseball players, which blunted my enthusiasm. I was hoping for more stories about famous females. Was Amelia Earhart the only girl in the whole world that ever did anything interesting, I wondered?

Week long stints with my grandparents were usually the case whenever Mother would have another baby. This was a long time to be away from your Mother and since the hospital did not allow children to visit patients, we pretty much had to sit out all the excitement and just wait until Dad brought Mom and baby home.

We had some options, however, if she gave birth in the St. Clare hospital in Fort Benton instead of the one in Great Falls. At the St. Clare hospital we could visit Mother from the sidewalk or lawn that surrounded the hospital, waving up to her as she leaned out a second story window.

There, Dad could sometime take us into the hospital lobby and Mother, if she was up to it, would descend the long, massive staircase for a short visit with her lonesome, mother starved children.

I had never ascended that forbidden staircase leading upwards into the dark and mysterious world of mothers and babies. To me, it seemed wrong, for the nuns to use that staircase to separate children from their Mother.

But it was also a staircase that finally took me to the forbidden second floor and a clandestine visit with my Mother. Of course, it couldn't have happened without my Grandmother who believed that her wisdom trumped all other authorities in the universe.

"Today we're going to see your Mother," Grandma announced one morning as we washed up the breakfast dishes. Grandpa and the boys had just left for the ranch and Grandma was already plotting our expedition to the hospital.

"Really? For sure? And the baby too?" My curiosity was immediately aroused.

"Well, I don't know about the baby, but I think we can get you in to see your Mother at least for a minute or two. But you can't tell a soul. You understand me?" Her voice lowered and I sensed that this was not going to be a routine, from the sidewalk, sort of visit.

Wiping her hands on her apron, she moved to the kitchen table where she drew out her plan on the back of an envelope.

"You see, your Mother is in this room, here," Grandma indicated with an "x" on the left hand corner of the envelope, "at the end of the hall." The door to the fire escape is here, right beside the door to her room. If we are careful, we can hide in these bushes, sneak up the back stairs and slip into your Mother's room. What do you think?"

I had learned in my short life, to always weigh the consequences of my actions. "What if we get caught?" I asked.

Scoffing, Grandma boasted that there was no chance of getting caught. "We'll just hide you under the bed if we hear someone coming. The sisters won't suspect a thing."

The danger and intrigue of her plan excited me. "Let's do it!"

"We'll try it this afternoon, after it gets quiet up there. I suspect the nuns will be taking a nap about then, and the new shift doesn't come on until three."

As promised, mid afternoon found us moving from east to west, across the back lawn of the hospital. Hesitating in the shrubbery, at the base of the back stairs, we calmed ourselves and prepared for the climb.

"Make yourself small," Grandma instructed in a whisper.

Fully exposed, and with stairs creaking we moved up the wooden stairway until we reached the landing outside the fire escape door. With our backs plastered to the outside wall of the building, Grandma peeked through the window and tapped lightly on the glass. To my surprise, Mother appeared and quickly opened the locked door

"Quick, get in there," Mom pointed, whisking us into her room.

Later, as Grandma and I walked the five blocks back to her house, I considered what the three of us had just done. "We broke the rules didn't we?" I inquired of my number one role model.

Grandma seemed to be choosing her words carefully. "Well, yes, I guess we did, but sometimes the rules just don't make much sense."

I pressed the point. "So it's O.K. to break a rule if it's wrong?"

Grandma considered. "Yes, but the hard part is figuring out which rules are wrong and which ones are right." Then she ended the morality lesson with a pronouncement. "And I think that seeing your Mother today was a good rule to break."

The most important piece of mail that arrived in my grandparent's mail box each month was the *"Coming Attractions"* flyer for our local movie theater, which, after careful study, was hung on the back porch, right next to the back door. Once I learned to read, I consulted it regularly, discussing with Grandma and Grandpa the various movies and the schedule for each.

"*'The Boy with the Green Hair'* is coming in two weeks. I just have to see that one," I announced from my perch on the stepstool parked at the far side of the kitchen.

"Well, we'll see what we can do," she promised, bustling back and forth between the sink and the stove.

"And *'Black Beauty'* comes the week after that. Man, I can't wait!"

"Don't forget the Roy Rogers movie at the end of the month," Grandpa chimed in as Grandma put supper on the table.

The positive attributes of Roy and his wonder horse, Trigger were discussed as we ate our evening meal. With prompting, they might fill me in on a movie I had missed or an article Grandma had read in one of her movie magazines.

My grandparents went to the movies so often that they had their own seats. At least it seemed so, since no one but Grandma and Grandpa ever sat in those two aisle seats when I went to the movies with them. The boys and I could sit wherever we wanted which, if we got there early enough, was in the front row.

With arched necks and eyes staring nearly straight up, we watched spellbound as the giant black and white images hovered over us. During the news segments or kissing scenes we'd crouch down beside Grandpa as he dished out dimes for popcorn.

The walk home on warm summer nights was nearly as good as the movie. Rested and relaxed, Grandpa would begin his teasing routine.

"Who's sleeping on the nail tonight, Grandma?" he'd ask as we strolled along under the streetlights.

"Not me," Butch asserted.

"He doesn't really hang us on a nail does he, Grandma?" A deep sleeper, Denny wasn't quite sure what went on during the night.

Before Grandma could answer Grandpa continued. "Sure I do. Soon as you fall asleep I hang you on a nail on the back porch."

It was my turn to challenge him. "Then how come we're always in our beds when we wake up in the morning?"

"Cause, I get up early and put you back in bed," he countered.

"Why would you hang us on a nail anyway?" Butch wanted to know.

"So you won't wear out Grandma's sheets," he laughed as we passed through the hedge, up the front walk and across the patio to the back door.

Sleepy and secure, I welcomed Grandma's attention as she tucked me under the covers of the double bed on the landing upstairs.

There were several things that worried me about sleeping there. One was the violent picture of a grizzly bear tearing up a campsite. This work of art hung on the attic door in the adjoining room, directly across from where I was sleeping. Day or night, I always closed my eyes whenever I passed that doorway. The attic door also worried me. One could never tell what might be lurking in an attic.

But I did not worry about hanging on a nail all night. Grandpa wouldn't do that to me. But I was never too sure what he might do to my brothers.

"Well, that's their problem," I decided as I rolled over, back turned to the attic door, and fell asleep.

Chapter 7 — A Dangerous Game

Sometimes, struggling to remember past events I can only bring a picture to mind. The framework and wall that supports the picture elude me. When was Butch scalded in hot oil? I can't place it in a time continuum. I think it happened before Denny was born but I'm not sure.

What I am sure of, was the horror on Mother's face as she ripped the shirt off my brother's back and screamed for me to get help. It seems to me that Grandpa was in the shop and I raced there as fast as my legs would carry me.

And then Butch was gone. Would he be back? Would I see him again? What would life be like without him? I didn't know how to ask these questions. I only knew that my days were empty without him. Gloom, like alkali scum on a stagnant pond, settled into our kitchen. Talk around the dinner table was quiet and subdued. Mother was not there to rock me or read me stories. Would my brother die? I wished I could ask someone that question. I really needed to know.

But there was one question I dared not ask. It was the scariest question of all. "Was the accident my fault?"

Mother had warned us several times about running through the kitchen as she worked at the hot, dangerous job of rendering lard. But the racing, squealing and laughter did not stop. Round and round we went, from the kitchen to the front room, through my parent's bedroom and then banging back through the door between their room and the kitchen.

"You two are going to get hurt if you don't stop running through here," she warned. "Go in the front room and stay there."

Zoom, back we came and off we went again, paying her no mind. And then, crashing through the bedroom door into the kitchen at just the wrong moment Butch ran straight into Mother's skirt as she lifted the heavy pot of oil off the stove. The blistering grease poured over his head and down over his shoulders.

"Run," mother screamed. "Get your Grandpa!"

Butch and Mother were gone a long time. It seemed my life would never be the same and it worried me that I was learning to make do without them.

Then one morning, as Dad finished his last cup of coffee, he called me back to the table. He picked me up and snuggled me into his big lap.

"Guess who's coming home today," he teased. "Mommy and Butch will be here after lunch. Isn't that good news?"

"Really?" I could hardly believe our good fortune. I hugged Dad tightly as two sets of eyes filled with tears of joy.

Dad continued, "You will have to be an especially good girl, Kareen. You'll have to be careful and gentle with Butch. He won't be able to roughhouse like he used to, at least for a while. And you'll need to listen to Mommy and help her when she asks. Can you do that?"

Does a child understand the concept of redemption? I can't say. I only know that I had just been given a chance to make things right and I was determined that this time, my Dad could count on me.

"Yes, I can Daddy. I can help Mommy and I can take care of Butch and I will be the best girl in the whole world," I assured him as I smothered him with kisses.

That afternoon Butch was carried into the house and put down on the kitchen floor. I examined him closely, taking note of the gauze and tape surrounding his chest and arms.

"Careful," the adults warned as I reached out to greet my brother. Gingerly, at arm's length, we exchanged a hug. And then, because we were very small and at knee level with the grownups, they missed what passed between brother and sister.

It wasn't a smile, but more of a grin with some devilment at the corners. With eyes locked, right there in the middle of the kitchen, surrounded by worried parents and grandparents, Butch and I understood that the fun, adventure and even occasional danger that we were so accustom to would soon be revived.

Danger was commonplace on a ranch. Hazards were everywhere. Mom tended to let us have the run of the place. Dad was more cautious. He warned us sternly about the everyday dangers of farm life and reminded us continually, to be careful.

"Watch for snakes," he'd warn as we headed off on hot summer days. "If you hear a rattler, come and get us."

"Kill it with a hoe," Mom would advise.

Killing my first snake was an earthshaking event. The men must have been in the field and Mother on the road somewhere since the boys and I finished the execution just about the same time she pulled up at the front gate.

Playing in the front yard, we heard the snake before we saw it. Shaking its rattles like a Marimba band on steroids, the coiled rattlesnake raised its head into the strike position, warning us to keep our distance.

Panic was our initial response. Butch and Denny screamed out a warning as I grabbed Jimmy, just a toddler, and pulled him back from the walkway.

"Rocks!" I yelled. "Get me some big rocks." In the same breath I screamed at Jimmy to stay behind me. The adrenalin was surging and I was snapping orders like a drill sergeant.

The boys began running back and forth piling rocks at my feet as I pitched them towards the angry beast only a few yards away. With lightning-quick striking motions the snake tried to set his poison into his attackers. Soon the boys were also hurling rocks at the angry rattler. Guts oozed as the rattlesnake finally fell limp and quiet.

Breathing heavily, Butch and Denny hovered over our kill, each with one more rock, just in case it was needed. Eager to do his part, Jimmy rushed forward with his own rock. Grabbing him from behind I held him back. I wasn't sure, but the snake could be playing possum.

It was then that Mother pulled up to the gate. All three of us began talking at once. Even Jimmy, rock at the ready, babbled his version of events.

Enthusiastically we recounted our courageous assault on the rattler. Leaning over the creature, Mother poked it with a stick. Nothing moved. It was dead quiet in the yard. I thought I could hear my heart beating. She poked it again. Still nothing moved.

Swinging Jimmy up on her hip she moved toward the house, complementing us on our quick thinking and right actions.

We felt like real heroes. Safety and serenity had been restored to the front yard and Jimmy had been protected from harm. Nothing could scare us!

"Better keep your distance for awhile," Mother warned as the screen door slammed shut behind her. "Snakes aren't dead until sundown you know."

Mouths agape we stared, first at her, then at each other and lastly at the snake. The thought of it coming back to life was enough to make us break into a cold sweat.

Several times throughout the afternoon, the three of us returned to the battleground.

"It looks dead," Denny offered.

"It's not," Butch argued. "I just saw it move."

"You did not!"

"Did too! There, see, it just moved again!"

Denny poked at the limp snake. I crept closer for a better look.

It was hard to be sure.

Before supper we took Dad out to see our snake. It was still there, dead in the grass, or so it seemed. Considering the sun's position, we warned him to be careful.

Bending down, Dad drew his pocket knife and with one quick swipe sliced the rattles from the snake's tail. Throwing the beast up over the wire fence, he passed the rattle to me.

"How many rattles?" he asked.

Carefully I counted the fingernail-like pockets that formed the rattle. "Eight," I announced confidently.

"See here," he showed me. "You missed the button at the end. That counts as one more. Nine rattles is a big snake. Good job kids."

Proudly, we turned to go inside, just as Mom turned on the lights in the kitchen.

One summer the shelter belt was declared off-limits. A badger had moved in. Even Mom was afraid of badgers.

"They're the meanest animal alive," she cautioned. "You stay away from there, you hear me. Badgers will tear you to pieces if they get a hold of you."

While I never actually saw the badger, there was plenty of evidence that this vicious creature was on the prowl. Mornings revealed dead chickens and sucked eggs scattered around the barnyard. With each invasion, the badger's size and ferocity grew in my imagination.

Good sense kept us close to the house but, as the days grew hotter, I resented this animal's intrusion into our shaded play area.

"What's taking so long?" I wondered. Apparently, this badger was smarter than most. He had already avoided several attempts to trap him.

Grandpa and Dad had tracked him to a huge mound of dirt near the first row of trees. They considered their remaining options. They could try digging him out but that was next to impossible since badgers could dig faster than a whip could crack. And neither of them looked forward to a face-to-face confrontation with a badger as big as this one. The dog or even one of them might get seriously hurt.

Patience, along with a well placed bullet, seemed to be the only solution. Grandpa volunteered to take the day shift. Dad would stake out the area during the evening hours.

Finally, they announced that the shelter belt was free and clear of badgers. We loaded up our wagon, grabbed a snack and headed for the trees. Tarzan and Jane were back in residence.

When we weren't playing in the shelter belt we were most likely setting up house in one of several empty granaries; in the barn, or under foot in the shop.

"Don't watch when I'm welding," Dad would caution as he donned his welder's helmet. "It'll make you go blind."

"Surely not," we thought as we watched the sparks fly and the metal fuse together

"Don't climb in the hayloft," Dad warned. "You'll fall and break your necks."

"He'll never know," we'd tell ourselves as we waited for the men to leave for the fields, then climbed into the feeding trough, up the ladder nailed against the side wall, through the hole in the barn ceiling and finally into the sun-filtered haze of the loft.

When the sows were having their babies we were warned to stay away from the pigpens. "If you get them agitated they'll eat their babies or you, if they catch you."

Stalking the wire pens was a risky game. If Grandpa or Dad caught us bothering the pigs it could be almost as dangerous as getting caught by one of those nervous sows. But danger was our business.

"Let's go see the baby pigs," one of us would eventually suggest.

We moved slowly and quietly through the pens, admiring the baby pigs as they snuggled in piles on the sunny side of the pig house or nursed at their mother's side. All seemed peaceful and serene until, for no good reason, a sow might turn homicidal, charging the flimsy wire fence with only one objective in mind; to tear us to bits. Terrified by the wild eyed angry huffing of a frantic mother sow, we'd run for our lives.

Dad was convinced I should wear shoes. "Why are you out here in bare feet, Kareen?" he would inquire for maybe the hundredth time. "One of these days you'll step in some cactus and then maybe you'll listen when I tell you something."

We were never very good at listening. Dad told the boys to avoid skunks but they just had to get a little closer. "I told you to leave them alone!" Dad yelled as he stripped them naked out on the back step and washed them down with soap, water and vinegar.

We had geese once. I'm not sure why. Maybe Grandma wanted a goose for Christmas dinner. The geese were cranky creatures, always hissing and threatening attack, a demeanor that drove Mother to complain, constantly, about having them on the place.

Violence erupted one afternoon as three year old Denny wandered through the back gate, out towards the chicken house. I was jerked to attention by his screams and Mother's race to the chicken house, axe in hand. A huge gander had Denny on the ground, fiercely pecking away at his face and arms.

With lightning speed, Mother was on the bird, swinging wildly with the axe, knocking it senseless and then killing it on the spot. Gathering her sobbing, bloody boy up on her hip she carried him towards the house.

"Get those god damn geese out of here!" she yelled as Dad and Grandpa came running from the barn. And that was the last we saw of the geese.

That's how it went, day after day. Dangers were eliminated or, at the very least, outwitted. While we considered the ranch to be our very own 'wild kingdom', we were confident that the grown-ups were always close by, keeping us safe and getting us out of any trouble we might find ourselves in. As children, we didn't know the meaning of real fear until one night when Dad was away at a meeting in town.

Montana could be a dangerous place when humans disregarded or casually ignored hazards such as snakes, lightning storms or blinding blizzards. Confident in the knowledge that Montana had never had a tornado, we were shocked, early one rain soaked morning, to find a granary lifted from its foundation and dropped down on the roof of the root cellar.

But when it came to our fellow citizens, Montana was the safest of places. Neighbor looked after neighbor. Town's people were trustworthy. A man could park his pickup truck in front of the Overland Bar, leave it unlocked, with keys in the ignition and a rifle in the gun rack, come back hours later and find everything just as he had left it. The residents of Chouteau County were basically honest and predictable so it was seldom, if ever, that people locked their doors. Some homes, like ours, didn't even have locks, which proved to be a problem that eventful night when Dad was away.

With our home located on a crossroad, it was easy to know who was coming and going in the Valley. Vehicles coming from the east or from the north were neighbors. Travelers approaching from the south or west most likely were neighbors heading home or they might be someone from town, or possibly, but unlikely, total strangers.

Because headlights coming from town after dark were rare, they were watched carefully. Traversing the valley's maze of dirt roads, especially at night, was something that only the locals attempted and since this was a weeknight, most of our neighbors would be home, or like Dad, due at a much later hour.

And so the headlights coming from the west caught Mother's attention. Casually she glanced from the kitchen window as the car reached the intersection. Perhaps they would turn north.

But the car continued past the mailboxes and through the intersection. That meant there were only two remaining possibilities. The car was either coming to our house or going on to the Cox place. The car did not pass by. Mother waited for someone to come to the door. She peered into the front yard, towards the gate. She could see no one. She went to the east window in our bedroom. Scanning the yard she spotted an unfamiliar vehicle out by the shop. No one was in sight.

Calmly she went to the silverware drawer and drew out several table knives. Going to the back door she stuck four or five of them between the door jam and the door itself.

We knew something unusual was happening when she called us to help her push the heavy kitchen table up against the back door.

"Extra insurance," she told us as she moved to the front door, jammed it with knives and then pushed the couch against it.

"What's insurance?" I wondered, "and why do we need it?" I was sensing that Mother was not as calm as she appeared.

Again she went to the east window. We bunched up behind her, peering into the half light that washed over the shop from the lone yard light. Just then we thought we heard someone on the back porch. We jumped off the bed and scrambled behind Mom's skirts as she moved cautiously to the back door. No one was there.

Mother went to the phone.

"Bill, there's someone prowling around outside," she told him in a shaky voice. She hung up and made another call. I knew by the rings, two longs and three shorts, that it was Coxes.

"Elmer, can you come down here? There's someone sneaking around the outbuildings and we're getting a little nervous," she told him. "I called Bill and he's heading home right now, but he wondered if you could come down and help us out until he gets here.

"I'll be right there," Elmer assured her. "You and the kids stay in the house."

We checked the yard from every window. All was quiet. Not the peaceful quiet that we were used to but a threatening sort of quiet, as if something bad could erupt if we weren't careful.

We went back to the east window in our bedroom. Cautiously we stationed ourselves on Butch's twin bed surveying the shop and outbuildings. The stranger's car remained parked in the shadows.

After a few more anxious minutes our eyes were drawn to Elmer's headlights as he topped the knoll, dropped over the hill and turned into our place. We watched as two dark figures suddenly ran from the shop towards their waiting car. Doors slammed and tires peeled as the strangers raced for the main road. Running without lights, with the dark as their ally, the intruders disappeared into the night.

Dad got home just as Mom and Elmer sat down for a cup of coffee. His arrival signaled that the crisis was over and all was well.

I didn't know about "tears of relief" at the time. I just thought it was sort of anti-climatic for Mom to be crying now that Dad was home and any threat of danger had passed us by.

Retelling the events of the evening, helped along with our input, seemed to relieve the tension she had been feeling and even, eventually, brought her to laughter and outright giggling.

Later, Dad and Elmer took flashlights to the shop where they found the welder, tires and tools stacked neatly at the north door of the shop. They surmised that greed had kept the thieves on the place just about ten minutes too long.

Nervous energy evaporated into sleepy yawns as Mom tucked us back in bed for the night. Pulling the covers up to our chins, her kisses seemed especially comforting. Solemnly, she helped us say our prayers.

Thanking God for keeping us safe was expected of course, but we were surprised by her final request.

"And forgive our trespasses as we forgive those who trespass against us. Amen."

Chapter 8 — *Getting Educated*

The schoolhouse was just down the road, one mile to the south. It had been standing empty and unused for many years, waiting for the next generation's children to reach school age.

Around the house and at family gatherings I began to hear discussions about reopening the school for the "girls". Eventually, I came to understand that I was one of those girls and Linda was the other. We were both turning five that summer and both her parents, Bill and Eleanor Meeks and my Mom and Dad had been preparing for the eventual education of their firstborn.

There seemed to be a change of focus around our kitchen table. Instead of conversations about grain prices there was talk of painting the school building and purchasing desks and books. School board meetings were attended by my father. The County Superintendent of Schools arrived for a meeting with Linda's parents and mine.

I was aware of the fact that I was at the center of all this activity and I wondered what would be expected of me. Going to school sounded important and exciting but was I up to the task?

Mrs. Garber was hired as our teacher. The Garber family had leased a farm about ten miles northeast of us. They had three kids who would attend school with their mother.

Bob was about seven years of age. Kay was my age and Alice was just barely four. There were some reservations about Mrs. Garber bringing Alice to school but, since her other two children made up fifty percent of the student body, it appeared to be a good arrangement for everyone.

The big square school building, planted firmly on a corner section of the prairie, consisted of a coat room with two doors; one leading to a full basement and furnace room and the second opened on to the space where I would spend the better part of my waking hours for the next five years.

A long bank of windows on the south wall pulled in the warm morning sunlight. New desks awaited seating assignments and school supplies. Books were neatly stacked on shelves behind the teacher's desk. A teacherage was carved out of the east corner of the room, encased by two flimsy walls with a curtained doorway which was designed to provide some privacy for live-in teachers.

Outside, behind the school, were two outhouses. "One for boys and one for girls," Mother explained to me when I questioned the need for two such buildings.

There was also a barn with stalls for four or five horses. Mr. Meeks stocked it with hay since Linda would be riding to school when the weather allowed.

For me, the school's biggest attraction was the playground equipment that had been installed by the county over the summer. There was a very tall slide, several swings, a trapeze, a monkey bar and a teeter-totter. The trapeze proved to be my favorite.

This was a whole new world; a world that called me away from my parents, brothers and ranch life. Maybe it was the emphasis that Mother and Dad were putting on my schooling, or maybe just some innate understanding of how things ought to be, but right from the beginning, I sensed that what happened on this little corner of the prairie would affect my whole life.

While Dad spent his time readying the school building for students, Mom took on the task of getting me supplied and prepared. She determined that I would need tablets and pencils and color crayons. A drinking cup for the bucket in the coat room was also on her list. The one she purchased for me was an ingenious little cup. It was made of metal rings that collapsed into one flat ring, small enough to fit into my pocket. All I had to do, when I wanted a drink, was give it one small shake downward and the cup would magically expand back to its full size. This fancy little vessel generated a lot of interest and also made me, for a brief few days, the center of attention every recess when we lined up for drinks at the water bucket.

Mother was also putting together my school wardrobe. There were trips to town to try on school shoes and winter coats.

But her plan to get me into dresses and long stockings was unexpected and I thought at the time, somewhat sinister.

For most of my young life I had been firm in my desire to wear blue jeans. I resisted, with some success, wearing a dress at every turn and on nearly every occasion. Now, with school as an excuse, Mother was planning on getting me into dresses on a regular basis.

She got Grandma busy making me two new dresses which I was forced to try on at various intervals. Instead of my cooperation, she was forced to listen to my constant complaints as she tucked and pinned the material, gradually and masterfully, conforming it to my shape.

"You're poking me again," I'd protest as she tried to get the dress up and over my head without stabbing me in the eye with a straight pin.

The worst fitting came near the end of the process when I was forced to stand on a chair as Grandmother meticulously measured the distance from the bottom of the dress to the chair seat, pinning the hem as she ordered me to turn three hundred and sixty degrees over a ten minute time period. I whined that my knees and calves were being lacerated by her pins and needles. I sighed and I slumped. I yawned.

"Stand up straight," Grandma would order. Putting on my pouting face made no impact on her. "And stop your whining. You should be thankful your Mother and me are willing to do this for you. There are lots of little girls out there that would be grateful for a nice dress like this."

"Well, I bet you can't show me even one!" I muttered under my breath. Instinctively, I knew Grandma was fast approaching the end of her patience.

Grownups often do not realize that there is a limit to a child's patience as well. Mine came when Mother enthusiastically dumped the contents of a sack of merchandise she had just brought home from the Woodwards Department Store, out on to the middle of her bed.

There was another dress, to go with the two Grandma had finished and were now hanging, ready for school, on the back of Mother's bedroom door. There was new underwear and several pairs of ankle socks. And there was the dreaded garter belt and long brown stockings.

"I won't wear those," I announced firmly.

"What?" Mother was playing dumb.

"Those brown socks and that garter belt. I won't wear them." I calculated that now was the time to put my foot down.

Mother could be stubborn too. "Oh yes you will, young lady. When it gets cold you'll be thankful to have something on your legs."

I was not backing down. "I'll wear my blue jeans when it gets cold."

"We'll just see about that," said Mother angrily as she stuffed the underwear and socks into my dresser drawer.

School started with me in a dress and ankle socks. Kay and Alice also arrived in dresses but Linda, since she was riding to school, came in pants.

The battle was joined on day two of my school career when I arrived at the breakfast table in my jeans.

"Kareen, go back to your room and change those pants," Mother ordered.

"I want to wear my jeans," I bawled. "Linda is wearing jeans."

"I don't care what Linda is wearing. You are doing what you're told and that's that."

Throughout the fall the fighting over my school attire continued. There were no peace talks and not a hint of compromise on either side. Mother, of course, maintained the power position but I had the edge on resolve and determination.

The battle came to a head when the temperature dropped and Mother got the garter belt and stockings out of my underwear drawer one cold winter morning.

I'm not going to wear those things." I protested. I left for school in a state of humiliation and despair with brown stockings tugging at the garter belt around my waist.

"It's like being wired to an electric chair," I whined to Dad, falling into the pickup for the short ride to school. "I'm just going to die if I have to wear these to school every day."

"Now, sweetheart, it can't be all that bad. Your mother just wants you to be warm and to look nice."

He didn't understand. "I don't want to look nice. I want to wear my jeans."

Grandma didn't get it either. "Maybe she'd like white stockings better," she suggested. She was getting tired of hearing about the ongoing fashion quarrels between her daughter and granddaughter.

I was steadfast. "No stockings, no garter belt, and no dresses. No! No! No!"

Mother was beginning to get the idea. Exhausted and defeated, she came home one day with a new shopping bag from Woodwards. Inside were two new pairs of jeans and two pretty blouses.

"If I'm going to let you wear jeans to school, they're not going to be your everyday ones and you are going to wear nice blouses, not shirts. When you go out my door you will look and act like a lady or its back to dresses, do you understand?"

I understood all right. I understood that perseverance pays off and a little whining to Dad and Grandma doesn't hurt either. And so, I went back to the trapeze, my crisp white blouse tucked firmly into my stiff new jeans, soaring upside down, back and forth, through the Montana sky.

The Garbers, uncomfortable with living so far from neighbors and having a house that was not much good in cold weather, decided to move on to greener pastures after that first school year. Recruited as Mrs. Garber's replacement, Mrs. Lozier would be focusing her full attention on just two first grade pupils, Linda and me.

I knew right from the beginning that Linda was the brighter of her two students. But my new teacher was patient and worked hard getting me off to a good start. The alphabet printed on big green cards ran along the top of the blackboard. Learning those symbols and their significance was my primary task. "See Spot run" and "Look, Jane, Look", were keys that opened the world of books to me.

Miss Dahl came into our lives when we entered the second grade. She taught me all the words to "Buttons and Bows" a favorite song that we heard continually as it spilled out from behind the walls of the teacherage. She taught us about love of country as we raised and lowered the flag each day. And she taught me about shame.

Miss Dahl was the sort of young woman that you never wanted to disappoint. Her loving and accepting ways caused you to work hard just to please her. So, it was with soul crushing remorse that she taught me to have compassion for even the smallest of God's creatures.

Grasshoppers were a constant irritant in the Valley. Maybe that's why I thought it was acceptable to pull their legs off just to see how they would cope. Or maybe, I was bored as I waited for my ride home one afternoon after school. Whatever the reason, Miss Dahl, interrupted this cruel activity with a loving admonition, pointing out to me the suffering I had intentionally inflicted on the insects.

Regardless of the circumstance, Miss Dahl faced it with sweetness and patience. When I protested her assignment of Linda to the leading role of Mary in our school Christmas play, she affectionately explained to me the reason for her decision.

"Mary had dark hair like Linda," she explained with one arm around my stiff little back, "but I think the angel must have had beautiful blond hair just like yours."

Gradually, my defiant demand for the lead role melted away as she assured me that the angel had a very important role in announcing the birth of Jesus.

"You'll make a perfect angel," Miss Dahl assured me. While I was unaware of any personal, angelic qualities, at least for Miss Dahl's sake and the Christmas drama, I gave the role of "heavenly messenger" my all.

Third Grade brought significant changes to our school. That fall, Miss Dahl married Mr. Allen, a young farmer who lived down the road from the school. Our new teacher, Mrs. Palagi was joined by three new first graders, all boys. Linda and I rounded out the student body.

Larry came from a farm a mile north of us. If we timed it right, we could count on his mother picking us up at our mailbox, saving us the mile walk to school. Brad, another farm boy, lived so far to the northwest that we had yet to meet and of course, there was my brother, Butch.

Sometime during the year, my new cousins joined us. My Uncle Allen married a woman with two boys; Roger and Ronnie, and moved them from St. Paul to a farm he had rented several miles east of our place. The coat room was now overflowing with smelly sheepskin coats, ear-muffed caps and random piles of buckle overshoes. Our teacher's time had to be divided between third and first grade lessons with restless, unschooled boys demanding the bulk of her time and attention. These new male schoolmates had taken over our quiet learning center like Marines storming a beachhead.

Roger, a few months older than me, came to school with "bully" written all over him. For no reason, except that he was bigger and from the city, he thought he could replace me as playground enforcer. The younger boys seemed to agree since they no longer listened to a thing I told them but followed Roger around like he was god or something. But like all bullies, Roger had an Achilles heel; a head full of curls which proved to be his undoing.

Understanding that a new day had dawned on the playground, Linda and I had been keeping pretty much to ourselves, minding our own business, until one day the boys circled the playground equipment and tried to take the swings away from us.

I could stand it no longer. This was my school and no city boy, even if we were supposed to be family, was going to come in and take over. I don't remember who threw the first punch but Roger and I were soon locked in mortal combat. It was only by sheer luck that I discovered the secret to counteracting my new cousin's wrestling tactics.

With my back firmly planted in the gravel and Roger's knee in my chest, I grabbed a handful of curls and twisted him off of me. I continued to twist with one hand and punch with the other as he screamed for me to let go. Now it was his back in the dust. "No fair," he yelled. "No pulling hair! Get off me!"

"You promise to leave Linda and me alone?" I inquired with another twist of his locks.

"I promise, I promise," he whimpered. Surrender was sweet but hollow. Roger and the boys began to play their silly games out beyond the playground, leaving Linda and me to swing and slide alone.

One winter day we were drawn to the far side of the schoolhouse by the boy's shouts and screams. Rounding the corner of the building I saw my brother, tongue and fuel tank, joined like a fly to fly paper.

"Roger dared him," Brad shouted as I moved in to examine the situation.

I could see that Butch was in a state of panic. His eyes were wide with terror, pleading with me to do something as silent tears traced a path down his frozen cheeks. At first I thought that it served him right, following Roger around like one of Mary's lost sheep, but then I remembered that he was, after all, my brother and ran for Mrs. Palagi.

Grabbing the tea kettle from the teacherage hot plate she raced to Butch's rescue. As one, we watched her pour warm water against the wall of the tank. Turning to steam, the water found its way to the ice gripping my brother's swollen tongue. With one quick jerk he was free, minus a thin layer of skin which he left behind on the fuel tank.

Blood gushed from his mouth, ran down the front of his coat, dripped past his overshoes creating a steaming red puddle in the white snow.

"Ooooh!" we grimaced.

"Aaagh!" Butch squalled.

"You'll live," Mrs. Palagi promised ushering us all back into the classroom.

Bringing order to a classroom dominated by young boys was a challenging task for Mrs. Palagi. First, she had to get Larry off her lap. Larry, the only son of doting older parents and nearly grown sisters preferred to spend his time, before class, with the teacher instead of out on the playground. As we all trooped in for morning lessons, we would find her trying to get Larry unhooked from her leg or out of her chair.

"Teacher's pet!" we'd jeer, but Larry was oblivious.

Each morning, Mrs. Palagi laid out lessons for Roger, Linda and me to work on independently while she instructed the first graders on beginning reading and arithmetic skills. At first, I found it hard to pay attention to my own work as the boys and teacher worked across the room. Linda, however, finished every task on schedule and expertly. She continued to get one hundreds on her spelling tests. Her arithmetic papers were always free of red check marks and gold stars gilded nearly every page of her Language workbook.

"Why can't I get this stuff?" I wondered. I knew one thing for sure. Since First Grade, Linda had always been waiting for me to catch up before we could move on to the next lesson. Seeds of doubt about my academic abilities were blossoming into full blown fears.

"I guess I'm just dumb," I remember thinking to myself as my teacher passed back another Language assignment, smothered in red check marks.

Perhaps sensing my lack of confidence, Mrs. Palagi helped me discover that I was competent in other areas. She introduced me to Madame Curie, Dr. David Livingstone, Gandhi and Catherine the Great. Geography and history were my favorite subjects. I came to understand why people in snowy countries built houses with steep roofs, and why people who lived by the sea ate fish and people inland, raised grain. Unlike nouns, verbs and long division, all of this made perfect sense.

Friday was my favorite day of the week because that's when we had art class. Each week we studied a new piece of classical art and wrote a short paper about what the artist was trying to convey and what techniques the artist was using that made the piece unique.

Finally, the doors to learning were beginning to open for me. It was exciting to discuss my new insights with Mom and Dad. Going to school had suddenly turned into a treasure hunt and I was eager for each day's adventures.

That is, until Mrs. Turechek arrived.

Denny entered the first grade that year along with two of Brad's little brothers and Linda's younger brother, Billy. Roger and Ronnie moved to town so we had a net gain of two at the school, bringing the total number of students to nine.

Mrs. Turechek was not an evil person. I learned that later in life when I worked in the same store with her. At that time, she appeared to be friendly and cheerful with adults. I think it must have been kids she didn't care for. Or maybe she hated teaching. Or maybe, it was the long drive from town every morning that got her into an uproar. Whatever it was, she arrived mean and stayed that way all day.

Butch, Denny and I went home every afternoon stressed but tight lipped. From the very first day, we were in trouble with our new teacher but, since we prided ourselves on not being tattletales, we felt duty-bound to keep the bad news from our parents. Sometimes it was Butch, sometimes Denny, and quite often it was me, that got on teacher's bad side that day.

A routine request to go to the outhouse could bring Mrs. Turechek's wrath down on your head. And her arbitrary deadline for getting back in your desk caused one to run all the way out and all the way back, with very little time for doing your business.

In Mrs. Turechek's domain, nicknames were not allowed. She insisted that Butch be called "Donald" and that Denny should be referred to as "Dennis". Butch, who knew that he had been named after our Aunt Dawn and was used to being called "Don" by outsiders and "Butch" by family, took the change in stride. Denny, who had never gone by any other name, resisted the change. Punishment, for what the teacher classified as willfulness, resulted in detention. Most of the time, if we walked home from school, we could hide the extra time spent in the classroom. But one day, when Denny was again staying after school, Mother came to pick us up.

We waited with Mother, outside in the car. Time ticked by. Mother became restless. Butch and I became tense.

"What did he do?" Mom demanded. We hesitated but she continued to insist. "Why does your brother have to stay after school?"

Finally she got it out of me. "He didn't answer when she called him "Dennis", I mumbled.

I could tell she didn't believe me. "What? Are you telling me this is all about his name?"

"Yes," I responded slinking down in the front seat, ashamed that I had tattled on my brother. Now I was sure he would be in even more trouble when we finally got home. I felt sick.

Butch came to the rescue. "And she makes everyone call me "Donald". If she hears anyone call me "Butch" they get in trouble."

"That's ridiculous!" Mom exclaimed. The car door swung open as we watched our Mother turn militant right before our eyes. With jaw set, she marched up the school steps, barged through the coat room and planted herself in front of Mrs. Turechek's desk.

"What's this all about?" Her tone was assertive and demanding. "Why is Denny staying after school?"

Mrs. Turechek explained the infraction. Mother didn't wait for her to finish before exploding.

"That's the stupidest thing I've ever heard. His name is Denny. D, E, N, N, Y. Not Dennis. That's what we call him at home and as for here at school, it's Denny from this day forward." But she was not finished.

"And while we're at it; it's "Don", not Donald. That's what it says on his birth certificate and that's what you better call him from now on."

Pulling an astonished Denny from his desk, she dragged him back through the coat room and down the school steps. Mrs. Turechek followed close on Mother's heels, shouting all the while that she was the teacher and that she did not appreciate her authority being challenged.

Tossing Denny into the back seat, Mom turned, stuck her finger in our teacher's face and told her, in no uncertain terms, that she had better not have to come back to this school or there would be hell to pay.

Getting in behind the wheel, Mother slammed the door and ripped out of the gravel drive without even a glace in the rear view mirror.

We, however, could not resist the urge to stare out the back window at our red-faced teacher. "Wow! Our mother sure told her." We exchanged appreciative looks. Maybe life at Pleasant Valley School would now improve. We soon learned that we were overly optimistic.

Our one room school continued to reek of tension and stress. First graders were forced to stand until they could spell a word correctly. Without help, there they would stand, totally mystified. Sometimes one of us would whisper the answer to them. Sometimes we'd get caught.

I noticed that Linda had begun twisting the lock of hair that hung down routinely over her forehead. She would twist and twist until her hair began to fall out.

"Don't do that" I'd remind her but just like the rest of us, the best student in our school was feeling the strain. I knew school should not be like this but I was helpless to make it better. Standing up to Mrs. Turechek only made it harder on everyone and buckling under meant we all lived on the edge of a nervous breakdown. At home, Mother and Dad worried about Butch's sleep pattern. He had started crying in his sleep.

A former teacher herself, Mom quickly identified the problem.

"It's that teacher," Mom proclaimed. But in spite of my parent's concerns we were not a family to give up easily. No matter what the circumstances, we were dressed every morning, fed and sent back down the road. The walk to school was no longer carefree but a test of our ability to endure.

Events took a dramatic turn sometime in early spring. The second graders had started a section on "telling time". As always, I kept one ear tuned to what was happening in the opposite corner of the room. All seemed to be going well. Mrs. Turechek's mood was more upbeat than usual so I relaxed and put my nose back in my geography book. As the clock ticked towards the noon hour we broke for lunch, crowding around the long, low table at the north end of the school room.

Butch and I found our seats on the back side of the table, facing the clock on the south wall. As lunch boxes snapped open and wax paper unfolded, the smell of ripe bananas drifted around the table. Then, his curiosity piqued by the morning's lesson, Butch asked a question that would turn life at Pleasant Valley School upside down.

"What time is it now, Kareen?"

Mrs. Turechek swooped down on me like a hawk on a baby chick.

"Don't you tell him, Kareen," she warned. "Don, you figure it out for yourself."

"I don't know how," he protested.

He had forgotten that you didn't argue with Mrs. Turechek. "Well, you are not eating lunch until you can tell me what time it is," she threatened, snatching his lunch box off the table.

A hush fell over our chatty gathering. Eyes were lowered and sandwiches nibbled half heartily. I tried to signal "twenty minutes after twelve," but by now the teacher was wise to my tactics and moved him and his chair in front of the lunch table, facing the clock.

As the hands of the clock approached the one o'clock hour we filed past Butch to our desks feeling helpless and downhearted.

Mrs. Turechek continued to intimidate my discouraged brother. "You just sit there and think until you can tell me what time it is," she ordered.

Two o'clock came and went as we changed activities. Butch remained on his lunch chair, eyes fixed on the clock. Recess came at two thirty. We trooped outside and stood around in clusters with no desire to play while Butch sat inside, hungry, alone and befuddled.

Three o'clock and still no break in Mrs. Turechek's will. And still no answer came to Butch's frozen mind as the hands continued to move around the face of the clock.

I worried that she would keep him after school. We were scheduled to walk home that day. Should we leave him behind or wait for him? How long would she keep him? Would Mom and Dad come looking for us?

At the close of the school day, eight of us left the classroom but not before Butch and I exchanged secret glances of despair. Planting ourselves on the school steps, Denny and I waited for his release. It didn't come.

"We better go," Denny offered helpfully.

"We can't leave Butch," I protested. "Mom will know something's wrong for sure."

Denny was the practical one in the family. "So, what are we going to do? We can't sit here all night."

I knew he was right. Something had to be done. "I'll just go in there and tell her that Butch is going home with us and that's that."

Denny looked doubtful.

Summoning courage which was in very short supply, I entered the classroom. "Can Butch go now?" I inquired meekly.

Mrs. Turechek's resolve had not weakened. "No, he cannot and you need to keep your nose in your own business."

I turned, tears of anger and worry that I had managed to hold back all day began to stream down my cheeks. I finally had to admit to myself that only grown-ups could handle this problem.

I ran the mile home stopping only to catch my breath or to let Denny catch up with me. Bursting through the kitchen door, I didn't wait for mother to ask any questions.

"She won't let Butch come home and he hasn't even had his lunch." I exclaimed, gasping for air.

"What are you talking about?" Mother demanded. "And where's your brothers?"

Just then Denny burst through the door. "It's not his fault, Mom."

"What's not his fault? What's going on?"

We explained the day's events. Mother left for the shop to get Dad.

"You two wait here and watch Renae and Jim. We'll be back as soon as we can." With that they climbed into the Chevy and headed for the school building.

There were late night meetings with parents, the school board and the County Superintendent. I worried about my dad who was debating the pros and cons of resigning from the school board. I worried about what was going to happen when we went back to school.

But somehow, the adults were able to fix things and Mrs. Turechek's behavior changed dramatically as we finished the last few months of the school year.

Talk of "renewing contracts" and "just cause", were beyond my understanding but from the tenor of our dinner table conversations I concluded that Mrs. Turechek would not be returning to our school next fall. Needless to say (but I'll say it anyway) I was relieved.

The students of Pleasant Valley formed a special bond that year. We faced a common challenge and weathered the storm as one. We stuck together when events threatened to pull us apart. We learned to trust the adults in our life even as we learned that some adults should not be trusted. We had gotten an education.

Chapter 9 — Triple Trouble

"You pull one more stunt like that and I'll send you straight to the reform school, you understand me young lady?"

I didn't understand. It's hard to understand when you're jerked out of a sound sleep and warm covers. What was a 'reform school'? I had no idea but by the sound of Grandpa's voice I assumed that it was not a very nice place. And why was he yelling at me? Grandpa had never yelled at me before; at least not that I could remember.

My mind raced. I blinked and rubbed my eyes, trying to focus as he marched me out to the lighted kitchen. Mom and Dad were sitting, glumly at the table, coffee cups in hand. Grabbing the collar of my pajama top Grandpa forced me down in a chair across from them and headed back to the bedroom.

I heard Butch wail and Denny bawl as they too were dragged from their beds and out into the bright light of the kitchen. Chairs scraped back from the table as Grandpa shoved the boys down beside me. Mom and Dad continued to glower in our direction.

Gradually my mind began to clear. I shivered; not from exposure to the cool morning air, but from fear. This was probably about the shingle nails we put under Grandpa's tires yesterday afternoon.

Butch and Denny, still half asleep, stared blankly at Mom and Dad and finally at me. I stared back, wondering if we could lie our way out of this and then decided, due to Grandpa's surprise attack, probably not. We had not had time to get our stories straight or fabricate some justification for our actions.

"Maybe I can blame the boys," I thought as I my mind shifted into self preservation mode. After all, they were the ones who put the tacks under Grandpa's tires. "Just because it was my idea, doesn't mean they had to do it," I reminded myself.

As Grandpa pulled up a chair and sat down beside my parents I prepared myself for his interrogation. Sharpening my wits, I began by feigning innocence.

"What's going on?" I asked sleepily, rubbing my eyes for added affect.

"Don't you play innocent with me," Grandpa warned. "You know darn well what this is about and you better start by telling the truth or you will be in a lot more trouble that you are now."

I abandoned the "innocent" strategy. Maybe I could appeal to Mom and Dad. Tears would probably do it. I gazed helplessly across the table, willing my eyes to moisten.

Mom scoffed. "Crocodile tears won't work, missy! You better start talking."

I didn't want to play it but "blaming the boys" was the last card in my deck.

"Why is everyone blaming me? Why don't you ask Butch what he did?"

A good offense seemed like my only hope.

"We'll get to the boys soon enough," Dad injected in that quiet voice he used when he was beyond losing his temper. "Now, what did you do to your Grandpa's pickup?"

100

I reverted to the "innocent" ploy. "I didn't do anything. I just told the boys about a story I heard on the radio. That's all. They're the ones who put the nails under Grandpa's tires."

"She told us to!" the boys squalled in unison. It was obvious that they too were now wide awake and intent on looking after their own hides. This was going to get ugly.

Real tears began to wind down my cheeks. Everyone was against me. All I was trying to do was help my brothers and now even they were turning against me.

It had all started the afternoon before when Grandpa told the boys they could not go to town with him. With hearts set on a night at Grandma's house, they continued to beg

Grandpa, who usually gave in to his grandchildren, remained firm. "Not tonight, boys. Grandma and I have things to do."

"Oh, come on Grandpa, please, pretty please," Butch pleaded.

"Ya, please. It's our turn," Denny chimed in.

They could be so annoying.

"No, and that's final," Grandpa said stalking off to the house.

With chins on their chests and kicking at the dirt clumps in their path they came to me with their grievance.

"Grandpa is so mean," they pouted. "He says 'no' to us all the time. It's not fair."

I listened sympathetically. "Grandpa has been sort of grouchy lately," I agreed.

Butch was ready to take action. "That's for sure. We should teach him a lesson!"

"How?" Denny wondered.

"Well," I said, eager to participate in any sort of conspiracy, "I heard a story on '*Inner Sanctum*' about a man and woman who wanted to murder the woman's husband so they put tacks under his tires. When he stopped to fix his flat tire they ambushed him and killed him."

"We're going to kill Grandpa?" Denny asked in stunned disbelief.

"No," I groaned.

"Shut up, Denny," Butch ordered. "You don't know anything."

I continued. "We could just do the part where we put nails under Grandpa's tires. Then when he has a flat tire he'll think he ran over something but we'll know that we taught him a lesson."

"What lesson?" Denny was still confused.

"That he should be nice to us," I answered impatiently.

"Let's do it," Butch volunteered. "That'll show him he can't be so mean to us all the time." Butch was not remembering that everyone considered him Grandpa's favorite; the grandson who could do no wrong.

The next few minutes were spent gathering up nails in and around the shop. We decided, or the boys did, that shingle tacks worked best because the nail had a wide flat head that stood upright when placed on the ground. The point was of medium length but straight and strong. It would be perfect for flattening tires.

Cautiously, the boys sneaked in behind Grandpa's pickup parked adjacent to the shop. I acted as 'look out' keeping one eye on our backdoor and one eye on the boys, ready to alert them the second Grandpa came out of the house.

He was taking his time inside and the boys had lots of nails. Wanting to make sure that at least one tire went flat, they continued placing the tacks under all four tires. Deed done, the three of us quietly faded into the barnyard like wolves into the woods.

So, now, here we were, around the kitchen table with me in the cross hairs. It just wasn't fair. Through tears, coughing spasms and the hiccups, I finally got out the whole ugly story. Loudly and often the boys protested but I plowed on. As I laid out the plot and the motive behind it, it began to dawn on me that we had done something pretty stupid. Sincere feelings of remorse began to filter into my confession. Sensing my change of heart my brothers began to accept their share of the blame and the kitchen was soon awash in tears. Even Grandpa had tears in his eyes.

With the morning sun creeping through the south window of the kitchen, Grandpa told his half of the story; about how, just past the school house, he had his first flat tire.

Just as we had anticipated, he thought he had run over a nail, changed the tire and went on his way. As he approached the Allen place he had a second flat. At this point he became suspicious. Two flat tires in less than five miles were highly unusual. It was also unusual to have two spares but he did and so, busied himself changing the second tire.

As his pickup ascended Vimy Ridge another tire went flat. Now he knew he had been sabotaged. With the pickup totally disabled, he walked back to the Allen place and got a ride to town.

He called Mom and Dad after he was pretty sure we'd been put to bed, warning them of his intentions. Together they agreed that we were the most likely suspects and that it would be best to present a united front in the morning.

Grandpa, who was normally an early riser, liked to take his time, have his breakfast and enjoy the morning. But it had been a long sleepless night so he was up and on his way earlier than usual; all the while dreading the upcoming confrontation with his grandchildren.

"Your Grandmother is having a very hard time understanding why you would do such a thing," Grandpa told us, as he concluded his account of events. "And so am I."

We sat with our heads hung low, silent and ashamed. We had no explanation.

Dad spoke first. "Do you realize you could have gotten your Grandfather killed? What if he would have had those flats going down Chinaman Hill? He could have wrecked the pickup, gotten hurt or even killed. What in the world were you thinking?"

"They weren't thinking. That's obvious," Mom said, making no effort to hide her disappointment in us. "It's like you don't have one full brain amongst the three of you."

Being sorry didn't seem to be enough but we expressed our remorse as best we knew how. "We didn't want to hurt you, Grandpa." The tears began to flow all over again.

Grandpa suddenly changed hats, moving from executioner to benefactor in the blink of an eye. "Are you really sorry?" he inquired gently.

Three heads bobbed like apples in a wash tub on Halloween. "Yes," we stammered, falling into his open arms.

"Well, it's not the end of the world, kids. We're all darn lucky that no one got hurt and the tires are fixable." Smoothing my tangled locks, Grandpa kissed me on the cheek, patted Butch on the back and pulled Denny onto his lap.

"I think you are letting them off way too easy," Mom warned him.

"Oh, I think they've learned their lesson," he countered. "How about some breakfast, Jean? O.K. kids?"

"Ya!" the boys cheered.

Relief washed over me. "Thank goodness," I thought. "No reform school for me."

Letting us off easy was not the normal reaction to serious childhood mistakes. Mom and Dad could dish out consequences like army cooks in a mess hall. And they had backbones like broomsticks. Begging and pleading for a second chance did not result in mercy, but quite often, just the opposite.

For months, I had looked forward to seeing '*Tarzan Goes to New York City*'. Grandma and I were the ultimate Tarzan fans. She had read and passed along to me many of Edgar Rice Burroughs books about Tarzan and his life in the jungle. So far, we had seen every Tarzan movie that had come to town and even her favorite horse was named Tarzan.

For several weeks, Linda and I spent much of our recess time discussing how Tarzan was going to operate amongst bridges and skyscrapers. This was a totally new twist to the Tarzan saga and Grandma, Linda and I were looking forward to being on hand when it arrived in our local theater.

Finally, there it was on the 'Coming Attractions' flyer; two big nights, Friday and Saturday, near the end of the month. I could hardly wait.

Grandma was going on Friday night and invited me to join her. Linda's mom said she could go with us. The excitement was building as the weeks ticked by.

And then I did something I shouldn't have. I can't remember what I did but I'll never forget my punishment.

"No Tarzan movie for you, Kareen," was Mom's verdict.

I believed she would relent. She knew how important this movie was to me. Surely she would modify her decision. Of course, there would have to be a substitute punishment like, "Alright, you can go to the movie but you will have to help with the dishes for a week."

"I could do that," I thought. I'd gladly trade a week of dishes for one night with Tarzan.

Or, maybe she'd say "You can go to the Tarzan show but you will have to miss the next Gene Autry movie."

That would be easy. Gene was beginning to look too old for all that riding, fighting and singing. My favorite cowboys were Roy Rogers and Rex Allen.

Consistently, as the days slipped by on the calendar, I reminded Mother that I was willing to do anything in order to see the Tarzan movie. "It's final, Kareen, and you might as well stop asking. You are not going to that movie." She was holding firm but I was sure she'd crack. I just had to be persistent and believe. I knew I had a kind and loving mother. She wouldn't keep me from Tarzan. She just wasn't that mean.

The big night finally arrived. Grandpa stood with me, hat in hand, in the middle of Mom's kitchen.

"Can she go?" he asked hesitantly.

"No, she can't" Mom replied. My heart sank. I cried. I begged. Mom didn't budge. Grandpa left for town, nearly as upset as I was.

I continued to bawl and wail. I stomped and pouted and then it suddenly occurred to me that there was still Saturday night. Maybe I should behave more sensibly and try for tomorrow night. "So what if Linda and I don't get to go together, at least I'll get to see the movie." I reasoned.

"She's just trying to teach me a lesson," I said to myself. I'll promise her anything. I'll do anything she wants. I'll be perfect. I won't nag her. Then she'll feel sorry and let me go." I just knew she would.

Grandpa didn't usually come out on Saturdays so I imagined a scenario where Mom and Dad would wait right up to the last minute, and then announce that we were going to town to see Tarzan swing his way through New York City.

As five o'clock came around I expected a call to come in and get cleaned up to go to town. The call did not come.

At six o'clock I reasoned that Mom or Dad would take me in to the movie and drop me off. So as to be ready, I put on a clean blouse, washed my face and combed my hair. But the supper hour came and went. There was no mention of going to town. Mother pretended not to notice that my heart was breaking.

At seven o'clock I knew the reels were rolling and that I could not get there in time even if Mother finally gave in and raced all the way to the theater.

Angry and dejected I went alone to the shelter belt and settled under my favorite tree. I tried to imagine myself at the movie. My mind struggled to fill in the gaps from the previews I'd seen in the weeks leading up to tonight. It was no use. My brain was not creative enough to go with Tarzan from the jungle to the city. It was over. In my whole, short life I had never felt so sorry for myself.

After a good cry, I followed the light streaming through the kitchen windows, back up to the house. It was hard to accept that Mother's power was absolute. If this was true, I faced a lifetime of suffering and catastrophic disappointments. It just wasn't fair. There would be no justice I concluded, only blind obedience on my part. This was a frightening revelation for an eight year old. I went, without speaking, through the front room into my bedroom. My mother didn't even once glance up from her romance magazine.

Corporal punishment was used sparingly; mostly as a safety valve for tempers stoked by too much worry or too much hard work. But occasionally, we got a good licking just because we deserved it. One of those times, when I knew a spanking was in order, was when the three of us got stuck in Grandpa's garden.

It had been a wet spring. We were warned to stay out of the mud which pretty much relegated us to the boardwalk that led from the house to the shop or in the opposite direction, to the outhouse. The front yard, which was mostly prairie grass, was relatively dry, but like the boardwalk, confining for kids who were used to roaming over dozens of acres.

After days of being consigned to the yard we began to venture outside its parameters. If we were careful we could jump from dry patch to dry patch, winding our way out through the barnyard.

It was serendipitous that we learned about the fun of skating in mud. Denny, being the smallest, sometimes missed the dry spots as he followed Butch and me, jumping like jack rabbits, down to the pigpens. Finding that his legs were not long enough to carry him to the next piece of high ground he shuffled along through the mud to the next dry spot. As we proceeded to the pens, he refined this technique and began sliding through the slippery gumbo, forgetting all about staying 'high and dry.'

Emptying our small brains of our parent's orders to stay out of the mud, Butch and I were soon following suit, experimenting with the phenomenon of rubber boots pushing through wet gumbo.

Step, slide, step, slide; it was fascinating to see our long smooth tracks tagging along behind us. But we kept bumping up against those dry spots. We looked around for longer stretches of mud; for a place where we could really get 'skating'.

We looked to our right, to Grandpa's garden; ten acres of idle plowed ground lay there before us; wet and welcoming.

"Let's go," Denny insisted.

"I don't know," I warned, "we're supposed to stay out of the mud."

"Shoot, we're already muddy," Butch argued. "We can't get in anymore trouble that we already are."

He was wrong.

Together we skated into the garden. At first the ground held but as we ventured farther into the garden we began to sink. We tried to turn back. The mud sucked at our boots.

"I'm stuck," Denny wailed as he struggled to pull his feet from the brown goop.

Butch tried to move towards Denny but the mud pulled at his unbuckled overshoes stopping him in his tracks. Reaching down in the gumbo, he tried to find the buckles and tighten them around his ankles. But they were stiff with mud and impossible to close.

"My boots will come off if I move another step," he announced with a hint of desperation in his voice.

My boots were tall and red with only a snap closing at the top. With mud caked hands I snapped them tightly around my calves and ventured towards the boys. Slurping at my ankles, the gumbo clung to my boots. I pulled first with one foot and then the other, wrestling with the earth for every inch of ground I gained.

Denny, totally immobilized, was now in tears. Still several arms' lengths away, Butch tried to keep him calm.

"Kareen's coming," he assured him. "Just stop your bawling".

But I wasn't coming. The mud got deeper, reaching half way up my boots. I was stuck fast.

"I can't move either," I shouted across to them.

Butch started to tear up. "What are we going to do?" he sniveled.

The prairie had us in its clutches and would not let go. My mind went into fast-forward. I pictured the three of us, cold and hungry, trapped in the gumbo for who knows how long. We couldn't save ourselves and screaming for help, if any one did hear us, would only bring very angry rescuers. There was no happy ending to this muddy adventure, at least that I could imagine.

Perhaps Denny and Butch were picturing the same fate as they stood locked in the earth's cold grip. The wind, ever present, whipped at our wet, muddy jackets and jeans. Our faces reflected the bleakness of the prairie in March as we pulled our coats tighter around our shoulders.

I felt helpless and doomed but I knew the boys still had hope. They had a big sister who was supposed to have the answers for situations just such as this. "She'll figure something out," they were probably thinking.

There was only one way. I would have to get out of this mud and get Mom and Dad. That would solve the gumbo problem but I knew it would create a whole new crisis.

"I'm going to try and run out," I yelled into the wind. "Then I'll get Mom and Dad to help you guys."

"They'll kill us," Butch yelled back.

Denny's bawling increased in volume and intensity.

My little brothers looked so pathetic, cemented there on the open prairie. I wished there was another way but I knew there was no escaping the dire and gloomy consequences of our morning escapade.

"We have to have help," I shouted across to them. Readying my weary body for an explosive sprint towards dry ground, I unbuckled the latch on my boots. With one gigantic effort I raced forward. The earth held tight to my boots, sucking them off my feet.

With one giant 'slurp,' I was free and skimming above the mud, with just barely enough momentum to reach a scruff of muddy grass a foot or so beyond the garden. With the boys and the gumbo behind me, I turned towards the house.

I walked slowly, plotting as I went. How could I explain our venture into the garden? What shading of the truth would convince my parents that events leading us into the mud were beyond our control?

I had no answers, no excuses, only a plan. I knew that Mom and Dad would go immediately to help the boys. That would give me time to save my own skin. I had contemplated running away from home at various times in the past but it always seemed a little too extreme. Today it seemed like the only reasonable course of action.

I had just passed the mailbox, heading straight west, when Dad caught up with me. What transpired in the garden as he and Mom waded into the gumbo to extract my brothers was never discussed and I knew better than to ask. But even with my eyes fixed on the horizon in front of me, I sensed that whatever had happened, had left my Dad in a foul and menacing mood.

"Where do you think you're going young lady?" he asked in an ominous tone of voice.

Brown tears trickled down through the caked mud on my face.

"I'm running away," I told him defiantly, pressing on down the muddy roadway.

"Not till you've had a good paddling," he responded, grabbing me by the arm and turning me homewards. "After that you can go wherever you please."

We stopped at the shelter belt so Dad could cut a switch with his jack knife.

Whack, whack; the sting of the switch reached through the mud, down through my jeans, stinging my cold, stiff legs. Pushing me up the road, we double timed it back to the house.

I could hear the boys bawling as we approached. Mom had stripped them to the skin and was washing them down on the back step. By the time she got to me the water had cooled and the March winds increased. She pulled off my muddy clothes while Dad dressed and then switched my shivering, blubbering brothers.

And then it was over. We were once again, dry, clean and warm and it was lunch time. Our morning misery was soon forgotten as Mom dished up the soup and I decided that running away was best saved for another day.

Chapter 10 — Pony Boy

Rhythmically, imitating the gallop of a horse, Grandma bounced her grandchildren on her knee; song and motion synchronized as she sang:

"Pony boy, pony boy. Won't you be my pony boy?
Don't say no. Here we go, off across the plain.
Marry me; carry me, far away with you.
Giddy up, giddy up, giddy up, whoa!
My pony boy."

While Grandpa loved his pickup and Grandma kept their new cars as shiny as the bottom of an empty dog dish, they were not willing to let the horse culture they had grown up with slip away.

From an early age, in the hill country of Idaho, Grandpa had plowed his share of his stepfather's wheat fields with a team of horses. One of his first paying jobs was as a stagecoach driver. Horses were used to break up the sod on his Montana homestead and helped generate extra cash in the lean years.

Grandma loved horses. Watching Trigger gallop across the silver screen was more exciting to her than watching his rider, Roy Rogers, belt out a western ballad. Her father had made his fortune buying and selling horses and cattle in the Idaho territory. Shires or Indian pony, Grandma had love and respect for the animal that had helped win the west. Horses for her were not a hobby; they were life partners, almost comparable to a spouse.

While Grandma could drive, she didn't do it often. Sitting atop her horse, Tarzan was where she felt confident and free. Tarzan was a big black Hamiltonian with a white blaze on his forehead. Grandma bragged that no one could ride him but her. Dad, who considered himself a pretty fair horseman, scoffed at that idea but I believed it to be so.

Grandma never wore slacks unless she was going riding and then she pulled out what looked like culottes from the closet under the stairs. The wide, skirt like trousers allowed her to sit a saddle like a man. There would be no ladylike, side saddle jaunts for her. With a reputation for being the best rider in the valley, she had an image to maintain.

Motorized vehicles brought a revolution to Montana. Spaces seemed to narrow under the big sky. Tractors and pickups didn't need to be fed and hitched before pulling into the fields. The rancher had more spare time and expended less energy earning his daily bread.

My grandparents were willing participants in this revolution, buying their first car in the early twenties. But, realizing that their generation was the last link to centuries of man and horse taming the wilderness, they set about passing on this legacy to their grandchildren.

"Never chase a horse," Grandma told me as we approached Tarzan with oats in hand. "Make them come to you." "Here," she'd say as she directed my hand underneath Tarzan's head. "Scratch him here. Horses like that."

At first I was afraid of the big beast. I had to reach high up over my head to find the spot Grandma directed me to. It was sweaty and warm underneath but he did seem to enjoy my tiny fingers working their way through his thick coat. Next Grandma put some oats in my hand. "Hold it up like this, palm flat out, so he can get to them," she told me. This was scary. Tarzan's teeth were huge. I baulked. "He won't hurt you," Grandma insisted. So I tried.

Big gray lips, soft like velvet, caressed my palm as he lapped up the oats from my small hand. My eyes darted upward seeking Grandma's assurance that he would go no farther once the oats were gone. Fear vanished as she gazed down, smiling and proud.

There were several aging horses on the ranch, kept on for sentimental reasons, as the place became mechanized. Dad usually chose Ginger if he had to use a horse for some reason. Beauty and Gypsy were used sparingly as they grew old, out in the pasture.

The only workhorse Grandpa had left was a huge Clydesdale named Diamond. Diamond had been retired from regular fieldwork for years but every spring Grandpa hitched him up to plow our huge garden. Both of them seemed eager for the work as Grandpa circled the huge animal, buckling him into the harness.

With "Gee" and "Haw" commands, Grandpa, reins in hand, followed behind Diamond, maneuvering their way through the barnyard.

"Get the gate," he'd yell out to whichever one of us was handy. This was the biggest gate on the place, wide enough for a team of horses or a tractor and equipment to pass through. Once open, we stood beside the gate keeping it from swinging back as Grandpa and Diamond moved through.

The earth shook as Diamond's huge hooves lifted and fell in the dust. With the tall wooden gate at our backs and Diamond's huge frame passing in front of us, we held our ground, confident that Grandpa had everything under control.

At the garden's edge he stopped to hook Diamond to the plow. Facing west, Grandpa clicked his tongue and gave the reins a snap across Diamond's back. As one, they moved forward with the plow digging into the black earth, turning it over in a line as straight as the horizon.

"Who wants a ride?" Grandpa shouted to us as he finished his first round.

"Me! Me!" we yelled in unison, racing over the newly plowed ground. Crowding around Grandpa we fought to be the first one thrown up on Diamond's back, knowing that each successive rider would be placed behind the first.

As Diamond, Grandpa and plow moved westward once again, we rode like royalty across a prairie fiefdom. It was spring and the meadowlarks were singing from the shelter belt at the far end of the garden plot. The air was crisp and smelled of growing things. Spring breezes teased at our hair as our backs warmed under the climbing sun.

Rocking gently, matching our movements to Diamond's lumbering gait, we looked forward to the turn at the end of the row. If, out there in the morning air, with the sweet smell of turned earth and in the company of a gentle, willing giant, we could have read Grandpa's mind, we might have caught a glimpse of the past and a way of life that would soon be gone forever.

It was Grandpa who decided we needed some 'kid' horses on the place. When I was seven or so, Trixie and Red arrived. Trixie was to be our horse. Red would belong to my cousin Roy in Spokane. Denny and Butch could ride him when Roy wasn't there, which was pretty much, all the time.

Immediately, Trixie became the prevailing subject of conversation in and around the ranch house.

"Why do you suppose he would buy such a mean-tempered horse for kids?" Dad quizzed Mother after a few weeks of dealing with our unruly new mount.

"Trixie is not a horse," Mom shot back. "She's a pony-horse cross. We'll never be able to do a thing with her."

One of Trixie's favorite antics was to take unsuspecting passengers under low lying fences or barn doors, scraping inexperienced riders off like peelings from a potato.

"Whoa!" we'd order, jerking back on the reins. Trying to negotiate a turn in any direction was impossible as Trixie simply ignored the pull of the reins to the right or to the left. Keeping her head down she headed straight for the short opening that served as an entrance to the cattle shed. We didn't understand her focus at first, but we soon learned that she was intent on dumping us onto the manure laden floor of the corral. Angry, frustrated and beaten we finally headed for the shop.

"That darn horse won't go where we want her to," we complained to Grandpa and Dad. Dad just rolled his eyes deferring to our Grandfather, who he held personally responsible for bringing this stubborn creature into our lives.

"You have to be firm with horses," Grandpa insisted as he walked us back to the corral. We found Trixie in a dark corner of the shed, patiently waiting for round two. Grandpa took the reins and led her out to the middle of the corral.

"O.K?" he asked. "Who's getting on?"

"I don't want to." Butch asserted.

"Not me," said Denny.

"I'll try," I offered. "But don't leave me!" I was fairly certain that Trixie wouldn't mess around with Grandpa nearby.

Grandpa lifted me up and placed the reins in my hand. "Now, let her know who's boss," he instructed. "Take her around the corral a few times."

I shuddered. The feared cattle shed loomed across the way. A weak kick to Trixie's withers and a hesitant "giddy up," failed to influence her.

"Go on!" Grandpa insisted as he gave Trixie a slap across her rump.

With a couple of crow hops she broke into a jerky trot. Squeezing my knees tight up against her sides and grabbing a hand full of mane, I went along. Like a passenger jet on automatic pilot, she headed straight for the cattle shed.

"Turn her, turn her!" Grandpa yelled from somewhere behind me. "Pull her head around! Get her head around!" But it was too late.

Trixie was once again safely inside the shed and I was on the ground. Tearfully I picked myself up out of the manure.

"Don't worry. You'll get it," Grandpa assured me as he finally turned Trixie out of the corral. He'd brought her out of the shed and rode her around a few times just to show me that it could be done. "Next time you'll be ready for her."

I had my doubts. "It would be easier if we just blocked off that stupid shed," I thought to myself, all the while pulling caked cow manure out of my hair.

Family and hired men watched with amusement as my brothers and I struggled to deal with Trixie's antics. Intimidation turned to resolve as the three of us tried to apply the advice offered around the kitchen table but Trixie wasn't called Trixie for nothing. She had a dirty trick for every day of the week and knew when and how to use them.

It would all begin with her resisting our attempts to get into the saddle.

"Snug her up tight to the corral fence, then climb up and get on," Grandpa told us.

We tried that. But one foot on the top rail of a fence and one leg over the saddle was not a good place to be if Trixie decided to walk off, which she did consistently.

"Lead her down into a ditch," Dad suggested, "then stand on the top of the ditch, get your left foot in the stirrup and swing your right leg over." That technique only worked if Trixie was inclined to stand still. Otherwise, you found yourself running sideways along the rim of the ditch, trying to rein her in with your left hand and mount with the right leg. Before it was over, you found yourself at the bottom of the ditch, watching the back side of Trixie canter off towards the barnyard.

After a while, Grandpa thought we should be able to saddle and bridle our horse without his assistance. The first step was getting the bridle on. It looked easy enough but once Grandpa left, Trixie had other ideas. Tossing her head back and forth she resisted the bit going into her mouth. Tossing her head up and down, she resisted the bridle going up over her ears.

If we were not too exhausted after the bridle was properly fitted, we moved along to getting the saddle on her back. It was Denny's job to hold the reins while I threw the saddle blanket on. Trixie would have made a great chess player. She strategized and planned ahead. Patiently, she let me smooth the wrinkles from the blanket.

She stood quiet and subdued as Butch and I struggled to push the heavy saddle on to her wide back. Calmly, she waited as I reached under her belly, between her four stocky legs, for the cinch. Pulling and tugging, Butch and I cinched the saddle into the highest and tightest notch possible.

Once Trixie was saddled and bridled, we stood back and congratulated ourselves on a job well done. We were ready to ride. Confidently, I stuck my left foot in the stirrup, grabbed the saddle horn and hopped along on my right leg as Trixie began to sidestep. This was a game of cat and mouse and Trixie was just about to pounce.

But I was no longer a novice when it came to mounting Trixie and so I stuck with her. Putting all my weight on my left leg, I swung my right leg over the saddle, searching for the other stirrup.

Suddenly, everything gave way underneath me as the saddle slid down Trixie's left side dumping me on the ground beside her. She turned, gave me a disdainful stare, pulled the reins away from a surprised Denny and trotted away to the far side of the corral with the saddle still dangling beneath her.

Butch ran to the shop for Grandpa. Again he headed for the corral.

"I told you to cinch her up tight," he lectured impatiently.

Pulling Trixie over to the fence he cinched her up again and ordered me to get on. Assuming that Grandpa knew what he was doing, I again got my left foot in the stirrup. Again the saddle slipped down Trixie's left flank.

"Well, I'll be dammed!" Grandpa exclaimed, cocking his sweat stained hat back and scratching his head. "She's bloating out her belly!" Determined not to be outwitted by this crafty dapple gray mare, he righted the saddle.

"Now watch. This is what you do," Firmly he planted both feet on the ground beside the horse's left side and pulled on the cinch with all his strength. And then, like the recoil of a howitzer, Grandpa's right foot landed a good, solid kick to Trixie's underside. With lightening speed, he next dropped the buckle into a notch three spaces higher on the leather cinch. Trixie seemed surprised, but resigned, at least for the time being.

"There! That ought to show her who's boss," he boasted as he hawked a stream of spit in the dirt and sauntered back to the shop.

As we became more confident and experienced with the horses Mother thought it would be a good idea to have Butch and I ride to school. I figured that the upside of this new plan was twofold. First, riding would sure beat walking to school and second; I could show Linda that I could ride to school just like she did.

But in my mind, Trixie was still Trixie and I doubted if she would cooperate with Mother's new plan.

Mother, as usual, never doubted. As the first day of the new school year approached, she busied herself, rounding up saddlebags to hold our lunch boxes and books; she walked us through the routine at the school barn, which would include unsaddling our horses, putting out feed and water for the day and saddling back up for the ride home.

Dad had our horses saddled and ready that first morning. Reveling in all the excitement that goes with a new school year, I forgot my concerns about Trixie. Both Butch and I were enthusiastic as we pulled ourselves up into our saddles, snapped the reins and issued a confident, "giddy up."

Turning the corner at the mailbox, we settled into the rocking motion of Trixie and Red's slow gallop. We were off to a great start. But as we reached the end of the shelter belt, Trixie slowed and then came to a complete stop. Red followed suit.

By now, I was used to her tricks and stubborn ways. "Giddy up!" I ordered in a stern, authoritative tone of voice, while at the same time, delivering a forceful kick to her mid section.

Trixie turned back towards the house. Just like Grandpa had taught me, I pulled her head around, back down the road towards the school. She stared straight ahead, ignoring my commands to move forward. I kicked her in the flank, slapped her on the butt, yelled, cajoled and turned her everyway but homeward. Trixie stood her ground.

"We're going to be late," Butch offered from the back of his compliant and cooperative mount.

"Just shut up!" I told him as I continued to try to move Trixie past the tree line.

Mother, who had been watching from the kitchen window, soon pulled up beside us in the Chevrolet.

"What's the problem?" she asked as she rolled down the window.

"This stupid horse won't budge." I responded half in tears and half in anger.

She confirmed Butch's prediction. "Well, you're going to be late for school. Tie them up to the fence post and I'll take you today. You can try again tomorrow."

I was mad all day. Trixie had totally ruined the first day of school and made me look like an idiot in front of Linda. "Tomorrow," I promised myself, "that horse is going to learn that I'm the boss."

"Don't let her have her head," Dad recommended. "Keep her pointed towards the school."

"Be stern with her," Grandma suggested helpfully.

Grandpa just shook his head. I think he was beginning to regret the day he had laid eyes on Trixie.

The next day was a carbon copy of the previous. Stubborn, stupid, mean, ornery, and cussed, were just a few of the adjectives that we were allowed to throw Trixie's way.

"It's no use," I complained after a week of failure. "She just won't budge an inch past the trees."

Mother was not ready to give up. "That horse is in for a rude awakening, come Monday morning," she promised me. "I'm getting you spurs and you're going to use them."

My shiny new spurs jangled as I swaggered confidently across the barnyard Monday morning. A new day had dawned. Trixie was going to school today.

As we approached the end of the tree line I prepared myself for a battle of wills. As expected, Trixie came to a halt. Butch backed Red off to the side of the road, ready for the rodeo he knew would follow. Trixie pulled her head around towards home. I pulled back. I urged her forward. She baulked. I swung my legs wide and brought the spurs down hard.

Dust flew as she crow hopped and fought for her head. I held on, pointed her south and kicked again. She jogged beyond the trees and broke into a gallop heading, for once, in the right direction. I pulled her back to a slow trot as Butch came alongside. We exchanged smiles as we heard a whoop from the grown-ups who had gathered to watch from a distance. For once, we had out tricked Trixie.

Eventually, however, Trixie won, because she made it difficult, and even dangerous, to unsaddle and saddle her in the tight quarters of the school barn. Trixie knew what she wanted and it was not hauling kids to school five days a week. It didn't take long before we were again walking to school, and glad of it.

We continued to ride Trixie, but always on her terms. Over the years we grew more fed up with her cranky behavior and so, it was with great surprise that we found ourselves falling in love with her sweet, good-natured colt, Flika.

Most of our horse adventures were just for fun but as we grew older we were expected to help with spring branding and fall round-up. By now, we had what Mom referred to as 'real horses'.

Dad, when he had the extra cash, enjoyed nothing more than surprising his kids with unexpected, super special surprises, and the three "real" horses he brought home from Great Falls one day fell into that category. Mine was a peaches and cream colored Palomino named Goldie, who had, in her former life, carried the flag in the Montana State Fair parade. Goldie was sleek, stream-lined, beautiful and best of all, cooperative. After Trixie, riding Goldie was like going from an old pickup truck to a new sports car.

Branding usually started early on a bright sunny morning in June. While Grandpa and Dad saddled the horses, Mom and Grandma rolled us out of bed, loaded our plates with pancakes and pushed us out the back door. They already had chickens boiling in pots on the stove and several pies in the oven but they still had lots left to do in anticipation of feeding all the neighbors and family who were expected to help with branding.

This was our first chance to ride and work beside our Grandfather. At long last it was time to climb into our saddles and move the cattle from the pasture across from the house to new grass in the big pasture, about five miles southeast, along the Green Roof road.

Confused calves bawled for their mothers as we moved through the gate and turned the herd eastward. Trying to curb our enthusiasm, Grandpa reminded us to take it slow. "We don't want to run any pounds off them," he cautioned.

We settled into our saddles at the back of the herd, savoring our role as "cow puncher". And there was a new skill to learn. As we moved along, Grandpa, who knew all of his cows personally, taught us how to attract a mother cow by imitating the bawl of her calf.

"Like this," he instructed, cupping his right hand over his mouth with his left hand cupped over the top of his right. Mournfully, he bawled away, moving his hands slowly, up and down across his mouth. Practicing kept us occupied as we moved along, with reins drooped around the saddle horn, our knees, pressing to the right or left, the only direction our horses needed. Wet cow pies dropped on the dry road in front of us, helping to settle some of the dust the cows kicked up as they ambled along.

When needed, Grandpa, with shouts and hand signals, sent us to the outskirts of the herd to bring a stray back into the moving mass of livestock. Confident of our mounts and our own abilities, we raced to the outside edge of the herd, swung wide around the stray and worked it back into the herd. As the morning progressed we began to react without direction, feeling at long last, like real cowhands.

Dad had gone on ahead in the pickup to open the corrals, fill the water troughs and get the branding irons ready. It was the beginning of what would prove to be a long, hard day for both man and beast.

Neighbors, as well as extended family members, knew they were welcome to join in the day's activities. Branding was a social occasion as well as an opportunity for the men to show off their skills with horse, rope and branding iron. The women while never too sure how many they would be feeding, enjoyed laying out their favorite dishes on the back of pickup tailgates and satisfying lusty appetites.

As youngsters wandered in and around the vehicles and horse hooves the older kids climbed to the top rail of the corral to get a bird's eye view of the action below.

No one entered the corral unless invited by the men who labored beneath us like gladiators in a Roman arena. The irons were hot, the cattle agitated and the action fast and brutal.

Rider, horse, and rope dragged wailing calves by their hind legs from the holding pen to wait their turn for the branding iron, ear notching and if the male sex, castration.

I wasn't sure if it was because I was a girl or if I was just softhearted but I had to close my eyes whenever the hot iron came down on the side of a frightened calf. But there was no escape for my nose or my ears as the smell of burning hides filled the air, along with the agonized bawling of the calves and worried pleadings of the mother cows milling anxiously around the perimeter of the corral.

My brothers and the neighbor boys did not turn away. As the men finished branding and tagging each calf they would call the eager boys, by turn, from the top rail of the corral to try their hand at calf riding. To the whoops and laughter of onlookers, boy after boy was quickly dumped in the corral dust by a calf determined to have the last word. It's ordeal over, the calf was finally turned out of the corral where it quickly joined its relieved mother.

The work continued as the day grew warmer and the dust thicker. It was Grandpa's job to get the number tags in each calf's ear, vaccinate and castrate. Grandma crouched nearby, recording the count and ear tag numbers as Grandpa called them out to her. She had two columns in her notebook, one for their calves which the men would brand with the AF Bar irons and the other for Mom and Dad's share of the calf crop that would wear the Bar L Lazy S brand.

Around midmorning, Mom and Aunt Dawn arrived with a car full of food. For awhile, they leaned against the rails of the corral; assessing the action and getting a headcount on the number of mouths they'd be feeding. As the sun reached its full height they set out the food. Towels that had been tucked in and around the boxes and kettles to keep the food hot were unwound and handed off to the men as they washed up in the waiting water basins.

As good as the food smelled and as hungry as we were, we knew that kids formed at the end of the line. With plates piled high, the men filed by us and settled themselves in the shade of their pickup trucks.

"How many left?" Dad inquired of Grandpa, as they crouched together, plates in hand.

Grandpa carefully checked Grandma's tally sheet. "Should be about forty, I'd guess. We're over half done."

Mother stayed around for awhile but soon she was calling me to help her load up for the trip back to the house. Packing the car with dirty dishes, pots, pans, and crying babies I was grateful that my responsibilities ended with a slam of the car door. Now I was free to return to the male's domain of dirt, blood, pain and violence.

Summer brought tranquility to the traumatized herd. The bulls were turned in and the process of making new calves began all over again. Undisturbed, the cattle grazed the breaks and hills of the big pasture directly across the road from the corrals. Occasionally they would raise their heads to watch suspiciously as Dad delivered a block of salt or fixed a stretch of barbed wire.

But mostly, they ate their way across the prairie and down through the coulees, switching the flies away with their supple tails. Each day, with calves in tow, the cows would wind their way single file to the reservoir. Never going directly uphill or down, they ambled along worn trails that encircled the hills like a fat man's belt. Slogging into the mud, they waded out into the water, drank their fill and returned to grazing. Their job was to put on pounds, and if the grass was lush and the reservoir full, it was a pleasant way to spend the summer.

Fall round up triggered another season of stress for the cattle. It was time to separate the calves, now referred to as steers and heifers, from their mothers and move them to market. Old cows were culled and would be hauled to the livestock ring in Great Falls.

Round up was a reverse of the spring cattle drive. Dad and Grandpa took their pickups while we rode our horses the five miles to the Green Roof road pasture. All day we worked the coulees in tandem with the pickups, gathering the scattered cattle into a herd.

It was the job of those on horseback to head off the stragglers and make sure we didn't leave any reluctant cows behind. Grandpa often forgot that he was not on a horse. Racing and bouncing across, down and through the breaks, horn blaring, zigging and zagging at every swing of the escapee's rump he chased the stray until it succumbed to the motorized monster and returned to the herd.

Once gathered, we attempted to restore calm to the nervous herd. Patiently and slowly, we moved the cattle through the breaks until we topped the hill at the front of the pasture. Mother had arrived, opened the gate and planted the car diagonally across the road just south of the gate to discourage any cow that might consider making a break for it.

Hanging over the top strand of barbwire, Mother counted the milling cattle as they bunched up in the corner. Four marks and a slash, then counting the marks by fives, she arrived at what she considered an accurate count.

"Only eighty-seven," Mom yelled over the bawling cows and idling pickup motors. "You've missed a few."

"Better count again," Grandpa suggested. "I'm sure we got 'em all."

Climbing up into the pickup bed for a better view, Grandpa and Dad did their own count.

"Eighty-eight," Dad announced without conviction.

"I lost one," Mom groaned. "I only get eighty-six this time."

Grandpa, who counted livestock as efficiently as the sleepless count sheep, confirmed Mom's original tally. "Damn! We're seven short."

I suspected that Grandpa was not as disappointed as he sounded. A few more hours out in the coulees, chasing down strays, was not such a bad thing and if the grandkids went along, so much the better.

"Well, might as well get them now as later. Get in kids," he ordered as he climbed into the pickup cab and slammed the door behind him.

Mom and Dad pulled up behind the cattle, moving them north, between the fence rows. Dismounting from our tired horses, we tied them to the nearest fence post and did as we were told. If the past was any indication, we knew that this could turn out to be the most exciting part of the day.

For country kids, who had never heard of an amusement park, riding through the pastures with Grandpa was akin to a roller coaster, tilt-a-whirl and bumper cars all rolled into one. Grandpa was notorious for his driving skills and never acknowledged fear or hesitation when there was an objective to be obtained.

His foot played impatiently with the accelerator, clutch in, ready to shift into first gear as Butch and Denny piled in the back. I dropped into the front seat with barely enough time to close the door behind me as tires spun and the truck lurched forward.

"Hang on!" was his only precaution as we headed east at breakneck speed. Uphill or down, the incline was of no concern to Grandpa. With eyes wide in amazement or tightly shut in fear, we held on!

As passengers, it was our job to watch for the missing cows which is hard to do with your eyes shut. Gradually, he slowed as we reached the back of the pasture. Denny and Butch pulled themselves up behind the cab and scanned the landscape.

"There they are!" Butch shouted. "Over there in the back corner."

"I see 'em." Grandpa confirmed. It was time to hold on again. With his right hand operating the steering wheel and jamming gears and his left arm banging on the outside of the truck door or blasting the horn, Grandpa raced forward.

133

With nervous stares the cows began to mill around and finally broke into a lope as they moved away from the oncoming pickup. This diversionary tactic only seemed to antagonize our driver as he pushed on the accelerator and swung wide to head them off.

The cows, now frantic, moved towards the far corner of the pasture.

"We got 'em now, kids," he exclaimed as he slammed on his brakes and deposited us out onto the open prairie.

"Don't let them get past you," he ordered swinging his pickup around back towards the corner. Butch went right and Denny left. It was my job to hold the center.

Grandpa slowed and moved closer to the cattle. They examined first the truck and then us, considering their options. We jumped and shouted trying to appear more intimidating than even we believed ourselves to be. The cows were not fooled.

Suddenly they made a decision and headed, at what seemed to be lightning speed, straight at us. We held our ground, screaming and waving like crazed fans at a soccer match. Just as suddenly they broke to the right.

"Head 'em off," I shouted to Butch, as my legs churned towards our right flank. Butch raced ahead, arms flailing and feet flying.

"Ya, Ya!" he hollered as he tried without success to get in front of the oncoming stampede. In a heartbeat the cows were beyond us, heading for the coulees.

The pickup skidded to a stop beside us.

"Get in!" Grandpa ordered and the chase began all over again.

Forgetting about his admonition to not run pounds off his cows, Grandpa continued the pursuit until the exhausted strays gave in and allowed us to move them towards the open gate.

Remounting our waiting horses we pushed the stragglers along at a slow trot, eventually catching up with Mom and Dad and the rest of the herd just about the time they made the wide turn off the Green Roof road down into Pleasant Valley. With the sun sinking in front of us I found myself daydreaming about supper and my warm bed.

My favorite song came to mind. I had learned it in the first grade but remained puzzled about the line, "pigheaded steers." At last, I understood.

My home's in Montana, I wear a bandanna.
My spurs are of silver, my pony is gray;
When riding the ranges, my luck never changes,
With foot in the stirrup, I'll gallop away.
When valleys are dusty, my pony is trusty,
He lopes through the blizzard, the snow in his ears:
The cattle may scatter, but what does it matter?
My rope is a halter for pigheaded steers.
When far from the ranches, I chop the pine branches
To heap on the campfire as daylight grows pale;
When I have partaken of beans and of bacon,
I whistle a merry old song of the trail.

Chapter 11 — Who Can You Trust?

"Mom," I screamed. "Mom! Hurry!"

Leaving her washing behind in the sink, Mother raced up out of the cellar towards the sun and wind at the top of the cement steps.

"What's the matter with you?" she demanded. "Quit screaming and tell me what's wrong."

"My teeth! They're falling out!" I was frantic.

"Here, let me see," she ordered as she stuck a wet soapy finger into my mouth and pried around the outskirts of my tongue.

Her verdict was alarming. "It's just your baby teeth. They're supposed to fall out."

"They are?" I couldn't believe what I was hearing. "How will I eat?"

By now Mother was laughing. "New, big girl teeth will grow back in." she assured me. "I should have warned you that this was going to happen but I thought it was at least a year away. I never heard of anyone loosing baby teeth before they're five."

She then explained to me about the tooth fairy that was in the business of trading coins for baby teeth. "You just put your tooth in a glass of water, set it in the window and the fairy takes your tooth and leaves you money." She made it all sound very straightforward.

But she left out the part about tooth extraction. Dad made a big production out of pulling teeth. I was placed on a kitchen chair, directly under the kitchen light while Mom got him a spool of thread. "Open up wide," Dad instructed as he made a little hoop in the thread.

He had me direct my finger to the loose tooth and then sit quietly while he poked the thread down around it. "It's just like roping a calf," Dad assured me. "Once I get the lasso around it, I just jerk and pull and it's out. Are you ready?"

Between the overhead light and the tears welling up in my eyes it was difficult to make out the fly specks on the ceiling. Giving Dad the nod to go ahead I squeezed my eyes tight shut and gripped the bottom of the chair with both hands. He jerked!

"Oops, the thread came off. One more try," Dad announced.

No sooner had my eyelids shot open, than he was making a new loop and Mother was moving across the kitchen to reassure me. It took more courage to open my mouth that second time but soon the tooth was out and I was running my tongue over the hole it left behind. And sure enough, the next morning my little white tooth had been replaced by a few gleaming dimes, nickels and pennies at the bottom of the water glass.

Mother didn't warn me about dentists either; she just took me one day. Dr. Sweeney was a warm friendly old gentleman with terrible tools. According to him, my new teeth were coming in soft and needed constant attention. The long, grim climb up the stairs to his second floor office was like a hike to the guillotine.

"How's my girl today?" my cheerful torturer would inquire in a halfhearted attempt at calming my frazzled nerves. It was hard to be angry at him so I directed my resentment towards my parents who brought me to this dastardly place.

"I'm tired of fighting with her," Mom complained as she tried to convince Dad that it was his turn to take me for a filling or a pulling or whatever else needed to happen in my mouth.

Helpless, with mouth agape, I endured the slow whir of the hot drill and the harsh blast of cold air directed at the raw exposed nerve of my diseased tooth. But all my visits to Dr. Sweeney were like an afternoon tea party, compared to Dr. Harshberger in Great Falls.

With Dr. Sweeney's retirement it became necessary, at least in my parent's minds, to find a new dentist. Dr. Hamburger, as I soon nicknamed him, was the exact opposite of Dr. Sweeney.

He seemed to me to be cruel and mean; a man who enjoyed hurting helpless kids dragged into his office, against their will, by sadistic parents.

"We wouldn't do this if we didn't have to," Mom and Dad assured me.

"But you don't have to!" I'd argue. "I'd rather have a toothache once in a while than go to that dumb Dr. Hamburger!" As usual, my fits and temper influenced no one.

It had been a particularly gruesome day in the dentist chair. There had been three or four fillings, several temper tantrums, some by me and a couple by the dentist. He threw his tools across the room, yelled at anyone within earshot and, at one point, kicked his stool across the floor with such force and speed that it banged into the far wall, rattling his Dental School Certificates.

"And he calls me a brat," I whispered under my breath in disgust.

Finally finished, Mother hustled me out of his office. I could tell she was shaken by the afternoon's events and thought it served her right. A good mother wouldn't allow their child to be tormented by such a mouth maniac, even if he was the family dentist.

We hardly ever spent the night in Great Falls but following my appointment Mom and Dad decided that it would a pleasant diversion from our usual routine. After supper at the café across the street we took up residence on the third floor of the Falls Hotel. Staying overnight in a hotel was a rare treat and especially welcome after my afternoon in the dentist office.

Throwing open the window my brothers and I leaned out to watch the people and traffic below. With neon lights flashing against the darkening sky, Mother called us, one by one, into the bathroom and then tucked us in between clean, white sheets.

With the muffled din of traffic and the glow of lights flashing against the walls of our room I found it difficult to fall asleep. Butch and Denny were already sleeping, balled up together like baby raccoons, on the far side of our double bed. I willed myself to lie perfectly still, enjoying the comfort of the bed beneath me and the excitement of night noises in the big city.

It was then that I heard Mother crying in the dark. The bedsprings creaked as Dad pulled her into his arms. My body remained perfectly still as I lay there across the narrow, carpeted space separating the two double beds, even as my ears perked up and my senses engaged.

"We'll get her through it. Don't worry," Dad whispered.

Always analyzing adult information I wondered who "her" was and what she had to get through.

Mother continued to weep. "I just didn't have the heart to tell her we have to take her back to the dentist in the morning."

I heard nothing after that except the wild beating of my own heart. I was doomed. I would die in that dentist chair. I just knew I would. Eyes staring wildly into the night, I lay paralyzed, frozen with fear and dread.

It was then, after a pleading prayer sent up through the neon shadows and the top floor of the Falls Hotel that I was given a new perspective.

I could trust my parents. Mother and Dad were in this with me. My terror was understood and even, to some small degree, shared. Finally I fell asleep knowing that Dad was right. They would get me through it.

The idea that prayer was available and had practical applications was gradually becoming a reality to me. It was comforting to know that prayer could solve dilemmas that I had given up on; like the time my tooth money disappeared.

Being a saver, I had accumulated quite a number of coins from the tooth fairy which I deposited into one of my unmatched white socks. Having my own source of funds gave me a sense of security that I had never experienced before. While I could now go to my sock for dimes and nickels for candy or ice cream my brothers, still in possession of most of their teeth, had to beg my parents for money every time we went to town.

Then one day my money sock disappeared. Of course, the boys were my primary suspects. Loudly and often I accused them of stealing my money.

"Kareen, you probably just misplaced it," Dad suggested helpfully.

"Stop blaming your brothers and go look for it," Mom advised.

Looking for it was a futile exercise. My small fortune was gone. Desperate, I turned to prayer. "Please God, help me get my money back."

I prayed because it seemed the only course of action left to me. Rightly or wrongly, the boys had been deemed innocent by my parents and all my searching had yielded nothing. But I prayed with low expectations. After all, God probably had better things to do than find my white sock full of coins.

Amazingly though, it only took a day or two for God to come through. Maybe it was just a coincidence that we got company and Mother moved us into her new room to visit. Maybe it was just luck that I was sitting in Mother's new red, overstuffed arm chair, but I think not. As my arms wandered down between the sides of the chair and the plastic cushion I felt something that did not belong there. It felt like my sock. Even before I jumped up and pulled off the cushion, I knew I had found my life's savings. It was at that exact moment that I decided that I could trust God with my money and my life.

During my early years I selected and discarded experiences and acquaintances as a produce manager might sort apples at a roadside fruit stand. Drawing my own conclusions about the character and reliability of neighbors, hired men and relatives was necessary once I decided that I could not always trust my parent's opinion. At times too forgiving or often times too harsh, their perspective of events, people and motives often differed from my own.

My long lost Grandmother arrived at the ranch with her checkered past and Mother's disapproval. After all, she had abandoned her family, run off with a neighbor man, and was now divorced for the second time. Three strikes were two more than Mother usually allowed anyone, let alone her husband's mother.

Her short visit to the ranch when I was very small is my only memory of my Dad's mother. She appeared to me, at first glance, to be very much like my full-time grandmother. Like Grandma Gallagher, she showered me with love and attention. She liked to laugh and tell stories just like Grandma, but in other ways, they were very different.

My Norwegian Grandma made the best lefsa I'd ever tasted which she did nearly every day using the leftover mashed potatoes. Grandma Gallagher specialized in what she called just plain old 'American' food. Grandma Swensgard, drank lots of coffee; Grandma Gallagher preferred green tea. Grandma Gallagher loved horses and the movies. Our long lost Grandma, loved to dance.

When the radio was blaring out music, she could not sit still, dancing across the green linoleum of the kitchen, alone or with a baby in her arms. If polka music was playing Dad or Mother was recruited as her partner.

"Let me try!" I'd beg from the sidelines.

At first I rode on the tops of her shoes but gradually I learned the steps, matching mine to hers and the beat of the music. Eventually, we fell exhausted and laughing onto the kitchen chairs. It seemed to me that Mother was forgetting to disapprove of Grandma.

Dad's opinion of my favorite uncle might in retrospect be blamed on the breakup of their North Dakota home when Dad was seven years old and Uncle Allen was eleven. Whatever caused the quarrelling and antagonism between them, I found Uncle Allen to be all a girl could hope for in an uncle. He coined a nickname for me and used it always, with a wink of his snappy black eyes and a smile that said "that's my girl." When I needed an ally against parents or brothers, I knew he would take my side. His teasing was in fun and never unkind. So, at first, it was hard for me to believe that Dad's distrust of my uncle was warranted.

Uncle Allen had not come through life as confident and good natured as my Dad and Uncle Bob. Life seemed harder for him to manage. In my parent's opinion, he drank too much and, since he looked like a darker version of Alan Ladd, attracted too many ladies.

Over the years, I found lots of reasons to excuse my Uncle's bad behavior. Maybe he had to grow up too fast when their mother left, I reasoned. Or maybe he missed his older brother, Adolf, who had died from tuberculosis while Uncle Allen was away fighting in the war. Or maybe he had seen too much as a tail gunner in the belly of a plane over Germany. But the most logical explanation, to my way of thinking, was that Dad had a family and a place to call home because sadly, my Uncle Allen could never seem to get his life on track.

Even when Uncle Allen finally got married and acquired two stepsons and, eventually, two boys of his own, building and sustaining a home for his growing

144

family never worked out the way others thought it should.

"He's always been a hell-raiser," Dad would assert anytime someone ventured to make excuses for my uncle's antisocial behavior.

Mother agreed with Dad's assessment. "What he needs is to quit drinking and settle down."

I thought they were too hard on my favorite Uncle. It seemed to me that life had not treated him fairly. I thought my parents should be more understanding. I thought I knew a lot.

Shortly after the war ended, Uncle Allen came to help out at the ranch. Even though Dad and Mom greeted him as a hero, with love and affection, they were cautious. Had he grown out of his wild ways or would he revert to his old nature? It didn't take long to answer that question. Before long, Uncle Allen's problems were affecting nearly everyone around him which, one dark night, escalated into what Mother called a "knock-down-drag out."

What caused it, I don't know. I only remember waking up terrified. I could hear my Dad and Uncle shouting and cursing and Mother's shouts. Running towards the dim glow of the gas light in the kitchen, I watched in horror as the two men rolled on the floor, punching and kicking with Mother trying to pull them apart.

"Stop it!" I screamed.

Fists paused in midair.

"Bill, now look what you've done!" Mom cried, scooping me up in her arms. "Allen, you can't come in here and act like this with kids in the house. It has to stop!"

145

Ashamed, with heads hanging like seventh graders on their way to the principal's office, they helped each other to their feet, apologized to Mother and spent the better part of the next hour reassuring and calming me enough so they could tuck me back into bed.

Over the years Dad spent hours worrying about his brother and his family, helping where he could. Eventually, Uncle Allen lost his family because of his inability to change what was wrong in his life. Drifting, alone and broke, Dad would find work for Uncle Allen on the ranch. Allen worked hard and was a real help to Dad but he never stayed put very long.

I continued to love my uncle and always believed that he was a better person than he let others believe him to be.   But I had to admit that Dad was right. Uncle Allen could not be counted on. Just when others needed him most, he needed to "tie one on."

Like a stretch of tight barbwire, their relationship continued over the years in spite of Uncle Allen's failures and Dad and Mother's disapproval. Always as distant and separate as fence posts, avoiding the barbs of hurt and mistrust, they would be forever linked by 'brotherly love'.

Mom's disapproval was a fact of life when it came to keeping our bedroom clean. A clean room was Mother's goal, not ours. My brother's goal was to get done as quickly as possible. They swooped up dirty clothes and toys like a shop vacuum, disposing of them in locations that would fool Mother's searching eye, at least, until they could escape out the backdoor.

My goal was to finish my latest library book. Whenever Mother assigned us a task she remained alert and watchful, checking repeatedly on our progress.

146

More often than not she found me sitting on the edge of an unmade bed, feet buried in dirty clothes and my nose buried in a book.

She would threaten isolation. "You are not leaving this room until it's spotless. Now get off that bed and get busy."

It was just such a scenario that led me to a disturbing truth that, perhaps, I should not have learned at such an early age.

As usual, the boys had finished their half of the room stuffing toys, dirty clothes and candy wrappers under their beds or in the bottom of our small box-like closet and were off doing whatever sorts of things boys do when there are no grown-ups or girls around.

Following Mom's orders, I tackled the most difficult task first. "I don't want to see a single comic book under your bed or on the floor when I come back in here. Throw out all the old ones and stack the rest in a neat pile," she ordered as she returned to the kitchen.

As I reluctantly gathered up my old comic books for burning in the outside garbage barrel, it occurred to me that some of the covers were worth saving and would make fine decorations for the bare wall adjacent to my twin bed.

Thoughtfully scanning the pile, I ripped a few of my favorite covers off my Little Lulu, Archie, and Wonder Woman comic books. I was standing on my bed, tacking the pictures to the wall, when I heard Mother's footsteps coming in my direction.

I knew instinctively, after years of trying to outwit her, that I should be looking busy. Jumping to the floor, I began feverously picking up my dirty clothes. The pronounced squeaking of my bedsprings must have convinced her that she had caught me sitting on the bed and reading once again.

"You're reading when you're supposed to be cleaning this room," she pronounced with all the certainty of a judge in police court.

"No, honest, I wasn't reading!" I pleaded; this time innocent of all charges.

"Don't you lie to me, Kareen. I've been standing right here by the door watching you," she countered.

What could I say? This was my Mother telling a big fat fib. I knew that kids lied, mostly to escape a punishment they assumed they deserved. But I didn't know that moms and dads lied. And the lie wasn't told to get herself out of trouble which might be considered fair under a kid's code of conduct. Instead, she told an untruth that would get someone else, namely me, in trouble. This was definitely unethical in my book.

I was shocked and dismayed. Life had suddenly taken on a strange, new uncertainty. I had always thought of Mom as my set point but on that morning, ankle deep in dirty jeans, socks and underwear, I realized that grownups could not always be trusted to tell the truth. I considered the possibility that, contrary to all I had been taught, lying was not always a bad thing but maybe, a necessary tool in life, called into use when others needed to be controlled or manipulated.

For once I did not argue with my Mother. She would win this round. Instead, I set about cleaning my room, thinking all the while about this surprising new twist in my learning curve. One thing was for sure. I would no longer succumb so readily to what might just be an adult exaggeration, a bluff or an outright falsehood.

At least with my brothers I expected that type of behavior, especially when there was any sort of competitive advantage to be gained, like the window seat of our family automobile.

The long drive to Great Falls was a challenge for my parents. Keeping four kids happy for fifty miles; five after Renae was born, required sharp wits and unlimited patience.

First, there was the never ending feud over the windows seats. I knew my brothers were not above lying in order to gain these choice spots.

"Kareen and Jimmy got the windows last time," they avowed loudly. Experience had convinced my brothers that Mother and Dad listened to the squeakiest wheel.

With my harried parent's fogged memories and in an attempt to always be 'fair' in settling this ongoing quarrel, it was quite likely that I would end up in the middle of the backseat, especially if the boys were smart enough to stick together.

One tactic Mother used to keep us occupied on road trips was reading the Burma Shave signs as Dad's Chevy whizzed by. If I was not still pouting about "always" being stuck in the middle of the backseat, I usually won that event since I could read rings around my brothers.

"Spring has sprung," I read as our car sped westward. *"The grass has ris."* Sign number three was coming up fast. *"I wonder where,"* I strained to catch the last sign, *"my boyfriend is!"*

"Shut up," I yelled as the boys shouted over my last line. I readied myself for the next set of signs.

"Around the curve," I read confidently. The next sign was coming on fast; *"lickity split".* Sign three flew past with just barely time to shout out, *"It's a beautiful car".* The last was just a blur, *"wasn't it?"*

Figuring that it was time to give Mom a break, Dad waded into the fray. "Who's going to be the first one to see the smoke stack?" he called out from the front seat.

Spotting the gigantic smokestack at the aluminum plant outside Great Falls was the object of the game. Once I realized that this was just another opportunity for my brothers to cheat, I withdrew from the competition.

Immediately, most of the weight in the backseat shifted as the boys scrambled to the left, back window of the car. At least that gave me more room as I slipped unnoticed into the right hand corner, at long last, in the window seat.

Grandma had told me all about the smokestack. She told me that there was an elevator on the inside of the stack that went all the way to the top. She told me that a couple had gotten married on top of the stack when it was first built. And most amazing of all, she told me that a team of eight horses and a wagon had been lifted to the top of the colossal structure and that the driver had turned the team and wagon around on the rim of the stack. I found this very hard to believe and told her so.

"They had pictures in the newspaper," she assured me.

"There it is!" Butch yelled. "I saw it first. Ha, ha, ha!"

Always competitive, Denny fought back. "You did not. You can't see it from here!"

I stretched my neck up over the front seat, scanning the prairie for the lone, dark pinnacle stabbing straight up from the flatland into the blue sky. Just as I thought; Butch was bluffing once again.

"Mom, make him play fair," Jimmy wailed.

And it went on like that until the stack was clearly visible and Dad announced the winner.

All the while; I prepared myself for the battle I knew would be coming next.

"Mom, make Kareen give me back my window!"

Chapter 12 — Finally, a Sister

"'Champ of the Week' at nine pounds, six ounces!" the announcer bellowed. Listening intently to the Friday morning '*Baby News*' on the radio I could scarcely believe my good fortune. At last, I had a sister!

But this was not my first sister. My first sister had been born five years earlier when I was only four years old. When you are that young, babies arrive unexpectedly. One day your mother is at your beck and call; the next day she's in the hospital and you and your siblings are dropped off at Grandma's house.

But, if you pay attention to grownup conversations as I always did, you begin to figure out that a baby has arrived. The verdict of 'boy' or 'girl' is announced and names for newborns are discussed. However, the only information I really cared about was when my Mother and newest sibling would be coming home.

But bringing my first baby sister home was going to be different. There was something wrong with our new little girl. As a four year old I could only listen as Mother and Dad discussed how Baby Lana would have to be given special care. Sensing the worry in their voices I kept my concerns to myself, locked away in the back corner of my heart.

"Would my sister ever be able to play with me?" I wondered. Listening constantly and intently to every mention of the new baby I thought I understood that Lana would never be able to do the things that Butch,

Denny and I took for granted. But maybe I was wrong. "After all," I told myself, "I'm little. Maybe I don't understand what's going on."

Then one warm summer day my fears were confirmed. Mother and Dad were talking about a train trip to a far off place called Rochester. Grandma and Mother were going to take Lana there to see if the doctors could help her.

"This is serious," I thought to myself. I worried about our baby dying in some faraway place. I worried about how long my Mother would be gone. And I worried about Dad taking care of us all by himself. I was more than worried. I was afraid.

One afternoon, sometime after Mother and Grandmother had boarded the eastbound train, Dad and I were on the way to town to pick up my brothers who had gone on ahead with Grandpa, earlier that morning. This seemed like a good time to ask the question that I was afraid to have answered, but had to ask.

"What's wrong with Lana?" I ventured hoping that Dad would not be put off by my curiosity and directness.

Dad seemed taken aback, but willing to help me understand.

"Her heart doesn't work right," he answered without explanation.

"Can the doctors fix it?" I continued.

"I don't know, Honey. I hope so," he replied with a solemn and weary voice. We rode the rest of the way in silence, both of us lost in our own world of worry and concern.

The news was not good from Rochester. Nothing could be done. Lana's little heart was too damaged and too delicate to operate on.

Grandma, Mother and baby were coming home.

The ride to the ranch from the train station, all six of us packed into the car, was laced with anxiety as Mother explained to Dad the doctor's diagnosis and the care plan they had suggested. With some bitterness, Mother also explained that Grandma wanted Lana moved to her house in town so she would be closer to the hospital.

"That makes sense," Dad offered unconvincingly.

"You want to move her to town?" Mom demanded in disbelief.

Gently he tried to reassure her, "No, I don't. But if it makes a difference in Lana living or dying we have to think about it."

Mother rode the rest of the way in silence. In the backseat, Lana's big brothers and sister were also, for once, quiet and subdued.

The days and weeks went by. We had wonderful times with baby Lana. She was beginning to recognize our faces and voices as we hovered over her crib. She returned our smiles with coos and giggles. Her grip was strong and resolute as she grasped our extended fingers. It was at those times that I allowed myself to believe that all was well. But then, there were the bad times.

For no apparent reason, Lana's sweet face would unexpectedly turn from pink to purple. Desperately flailing her little arms and legs, she gasped for breath, her eyes wide, pleading for our help. Screaming for Mother we recoiled from the crib, making way as she swept Lana up into her arms. Holding her close, Mother soothed Lana with quiet, loving baby talk and lullabies as she paced back and forth across the green linoleum of the kitchen. Gradually Lana's gasping would be replaced with soft whimpers and a deep, peaceful sleep.

After one particularly desperate bout, Mother finally gave in to Grandma's insistence that the baby be moved to town. The little baby bed was loaded into the back of Grandpa's pickup. Diapers, bottles and lotion were packed into a box and placed on the front seat of the pickup. With Dad driving the car, Butch, Denny and me in the back and Mother holding Lana, we fell in behind the pickup, covering the twelve miles to town, without a word spoken between us.

The ride home has disappeared from memory but moving Lana into Grandmother's house was a sad and wrenching event no one would soon forget. Mother was sullen and grim. Grandma was prepared and ready to take over. Dad and Grandpa followed orders, unwilling to add any more stress to an already tense situation. Me and the boys kept quiet and out of the way.

Emptiness settled into the ranch house as if we had already lost our baby. Mother's daily trips to town were now part of our everyday routine as Dad worked to finish up the fall seeding.

"She's taking over just like she always does," Mother complained to Dad. "She acts like Lana is her baby instead of mine."

Bitterness and pain were building to the breaking point as Mother struggled with doing what she knew was best for baby Lana and her growing feelings of

156

resentment towards her own Mother's assertive personality.

And then, suddenly, Lana was gone. A late night race to the hospital could not save her. I was too young to understand the guilt and recriminations that smoldered like a half dead campfire in the center of our family circle as funeral arrangements were made.

Grandma insisted that Lana should be buried at the mausoleum; close to the crypt she and Grandpa had already purchased for themselves. Grandmother chose the coffin, arranged for the flowers and even hired a photographer to take Lana's picture, as if she were sleeping. Mother selected the delicate little dress and pink bunting that Lana would be laid out in. And she chose the music. The soothing strains of 'Brahms's Lullaby' would comfort her baby in her eternal sleep, just as it brought consolation to Mother as she rocked and sang to her remaining babies and as she would to her babies yet unborn.

Our parents and grandparents returned from the funeral, drained and weary. The last four months had not only been exhausting and heartbreaking but had opened up an emotional chasm between our two families as wide and as desolate as the Missouri River breaks. While cloaked in politeness, so as not to affect the family and work on the ranch, the wound ran deep and would impacted our lives for years to come.

But now there was Christmas to deal with and three little ones eagerly looking forward to Santa Claus' arrival. Putting their grief aside, Mother and Dad immersed themselves in holiday preparations.

A renewed sense of joy permeated the evening as Dad brought in the Christmas tree and erected it in our front room. While he wrestled with the tangled web of new fangled electric lights, the boys and I raced from the cardboard box full of ornaments to the tall green spruce, hanging tinsel and balls in a slap-dash fashion. And then, without warning, silence and sadness made an unexpected return visit to our home.

All eyes turned to Mother. With tears coursing down her cheeks she carefully removed the angel from its box. Fragile, with golden wings, rosy cheeks and blonde locks, the angel was a visual reminder of our missing baby girl. With tears in my own eyes, I watched as Dad took the angel from Mother and placed it high up on top of the Christmas tree.

For some reason I woke early the following morning. Lying there, beneath my warm blankets, I considered praying. Being four years old I didn't understand what praying was or how you went about it but it seemed to me that I needed to talk to the Christmas angel.

Silently, I slipped out of bed and around the corner to the front room.

Early morning light was playing off the tree decorations causing the whole room to feel like the inside of a kaleidoscope. With sparkle and shine dancing all around me, I settled, cross legged on the cold linoleum, head turned upwards, gazing at the angel high up by the ceiling.

"Please take care of my baby Lana," I pleaded. "And", I added, " Mom and Dad too."

I had hoped that I could appeal to the angel like a big girl, without tears, but it was no use. Without bidding, tears began to drip from my cheeks to my pajamas and to the floor beyond.

It was then that I heard my parent's bedroom door creak open. I considered scrambling back to my bed but it was too late. In a heartbeat, Dad was crouched down beside me.

"What's wrong, sweetie? What are you doing up so early?" Dad whispered as he pulled me into his lap. Snuggling into his warmth and wiping away my tears, I explained my morning mission and how I was asking the angel to take care of us and Lana.

I have no recollection of his words, only his reaction. Pulling me even closer, we remained there together on the cold floor, as the light and promise of a new day filled our living room.

The following summer, another baby arrived, born, unbelievably, on Lana's birthday. I considered this precious bundle of brown curls an answer to my prayer but the angel made one major mistake. This baby was a boy. And so, I resigned myself to forever being outnumbered by brothers.

"Just as well," I told myself, "as long as they don't forget whose boss."

Mother and Dad decided that Butch, Denny and I should have the honor of naming the new baby. After some serious discussions and a few arguments we relayed our decision to Mother in the hospital. Within days, she brought Baby Jim home to us.

Jimmy was a delight. Cuddly, cheerful and beautiful, he spent his toddler time, tagging along with us everywhere his sturdy little legs could take him. Our favorite game was pretending to scare him with growls and snarls, as he ran terrified to one of us for protection.

"You're going to make that child a nervous wreck," Mom cautioned us.

"But he's so sweet," I'd argue. "We just can't stop hugging him."

"Well, you know you can hug him without scaring him half to death," she reminded us.

As he grew older, Jimmy found new interests. Playing trucks with the big boys replaced looking at books with his sister. More and more he tagged along behind Butch and Denny, learning the ins and outs of ranch life from the male point of view.

Any sense of loss I might have been feeling was lessened by my enrollment in kindergarten. I now had a life of my own, which was a good thing since the house, the yard and the fields beyond, were being taken over by three, noisy, quarrelsome, obnoxious boys who did not listen or respond to my direction as faithfully as they had in the past. Going to school gave me a new purpose as well as a respite from the percolating male testosterone.

And then, out of the blue, five years after I had lost my one and only little sister and four years after boy baby number three joined our family, there were rumors of a new baby on the way.

I had long ago resigned myself to living my life without a sister and so I did not look forward to the birth with any real interest or excitement. I decided that one more brother would have little impact on my busy life.

"Whatever," I told myself and anyone else who might be interested. "Who needs another baby around here anyway?"

And so, when Dad called Grandma's house to announce that we had a healthy baby girl, I had some real soul searching to do.

Instinctively, I knew that this little sister would not be the companion that I had been hoping for many years earlier. After all, I was nine years old now and what would we have in common? There were also family issues to consider.

Would she replace me as Daddy's girl? Would Mother love her more than me? Probably the boys would like her better too, since I had been so mean to them lately. Considering all of these possibilities was sort of like feeling the earth shake under your feet and wondering if it was going to open up and swallow you whole.

Joining Grandma at her kitchen table I voiced my concerns. Grandma, always a good listener, steered my heart towards the positive aspects of sisterhood. She told me about the house full of girls she had grown up with and the love and friendship they shared as they married, raised children and grew old together.

Before long, I was eagerly looking forward to my life with another girl in the house.

"She can share my room," I offered.

"And you can take her to the library when she gets a little older," Grandma suggested. "And teach her how to ride a horse and a bike."

"Did Dad say what her name was going to be?" I asked, now genuinely interested in our newest family member.

"I think they've settled on "Renae Ilene," she responded.

"Renae." I rolled it around on my tongue a few times. "I like it!" And I was beginning to really like the idea of having a sister.

Dad picked us up from Grandma's house that evening. As we got ready for school the following morning, Dad tuned the radio to KMON so we could listen to the weekly broadcast of births at the Columbus hospital in Great Falls.

Gathered around the radio in the kitchen, we waited impatiently as one after another, babies, with names, length, pounds and parentage were announced. "What about Renae?" I inquired of Dad.

He signaled silence with a touch of his finger to his lips. "Shss, they'll get to her. Just wait."

And then with a drum roll, they announced the 'Champ of the Week' and it was my baby sister. Next came the announcement of prizes awarded to the 'Champ' by the sponsoring pharmacy. My school blouse buttons were bursting with pride. Renae Ilene wasn't even home yet and already she was a winner!

As the boys and I walked to school that morning, I contemplated the bragging rights I could inflict on our classmates. Especially Linda, since like me, she had never known anything but male siblings.

But the best part was when Mother brought Renae home and placed her in the little crib. This was the same small crib that had welcomed all of us into the family; the same crib that had held Lana those four short months so long ago. But now, we paid no attention to Mother's warnings to be careful with the baby. This little girl could handle our roughhousing and teasing.

Wheeling Renae and the crib through the house, banging off door jams and bumping into furniture, Renae joined in our fun, filling the house once again with a baby's giggles and squeals.

But in quiet times, when I was alone with my thoughts, my heart went back to my lost baby sister and all that life might have been if she had been allowed to stay with us. And then I would recall my Christmas angel and how she had kept faith with me over the years, adding, beyond measure, love and blessings to our family. By now, I knew the difference between praying to a Christmas tree angel and God but occasionally, I felt compelled to send a heartfelt thank you to the rosy cheeked, curly haired cherub tucked away in a cardboard box filled with last year's Christmas decorations.

"Thank you, Angel, for listening. And thank you for my baby sister; my very own little 'Champ of the Week'.

Chapter 13 —Mud and Daffodils

Weather dictated life in Pleasant Valley. If it was dry, Dad worked the summer fallow. Blizzards kept us close to the stove and if it rained we went to town with hope in our pocket and smiles on our faces.

A 'good year' meant a snow cover for the winter wheat that had been planted the fall before; a slow melt in March to provide sub-moisture for the seeding of spring crops in April, followed by rains in May and early June which caused the seeded crops to turn the valley into a patchwork quilt of alternating strips of brilliant green and rich brown earth. The hot, dry days of July gradually turned the green wheat crop into waves of golden grain ready for harvest in the early days of August. September found the tractors and equipment back in the fields, this time, planting seed into the idle brown strips, thus beginning a new cycle for next year's crop.

Such years, while the hope of all farmers in the valley, were rare. Winters could be brutally cold but devoid of snow cover which often caused the winter wheat to 'freeze out'. Often time's tractor and operator were enveloped in dust clouds as worried farmers seeded spring crops, betting, hoping, the rains would come. Occasionally, late spring storms would bring cold and snow, causing the calves to freeze as they dropped from their mother's wombs. Pity the rancher with a good crop in the making. He would live in agony all summer long, surveying every dark cloud, praying that it did not contain a farmer's worst nightmare; hail.

Hail could be devastating. The wheat rancher's income came once a year when he hauled his newly harvested grain to the elevator and was cut a check on the spot. If hail got to the crop before he did, payday would be cancelled or at least reduced. If hail came in June, before the crop was ripe, it could turn a field into green mush. Even small hail, if it came with enough force and just before harvest, would shred the heads and pound the kernels into the ground. Hail insurance became an expensive shield for the farmer unwilling to risk his family's future on the whims of nature. But then, if hail did strike, there would be the adjuster to deal with.

A phone call from the unfortunate farmer triggered a trip to the hail damaged fields by the local insurance man and the adjuster. Thoughtfully walking across the muddy ground, they kicked at the mangled stalks, occasionally stooping over to survey the thrashed grain driven into the gumbo by the force of the hail. The farmer shadows their every move, hoping for a generous, or at the very least, a realistic appraisal. The insurance man, who sold the policy to the farmer and collected a hefty commission, is just hoping everyone will stay calm.

"Forty percent," the adjuster announces after some complex figuring on his clipboard.

"Forty percent? You must be joking," the farmer retorts angrily.

The adjuster was sticking to his guns. "Nope, you get a little rain and this crop will come right back. Hell, you'll probably make money on the deal."

Making money was not what most farmers did best. In addition to hail and drought there were other extenuating circumstances. Insects, cheat grass, wild oats, equipment breakdowns, low grain prices and high shipping costs all conspired to keep his hard earned dollars flowing into someone else's coffers.

Weather also dictated the activities and challenges of farm kids. Outdoor games were modified or invented to accommodate weather related conditions. Spring winds brought out the kites. Hot summer days might find us playing Tarzan in the shelter belt and in late fall, tumbleweeds, stacked three or four high served as a cave for make believe cave dwellers. Winter, unless sub zero, also found us outside.

Prairies, being by definition flat, were not the best place for sledding. The addition of a good strong wind to a snow storm, however, created drifts, sometimes six or more feet high. One particular winter, snowdrifts had piled up around our empty pigpens, creating a wonderland of hills and gullies.

Butch, Denny and I drug our sleds to the tops of the pig house roofs and flew down the drifts as if we were bobsledders in the Olympics. The rides were short and the endings abrupt, but by the time Mother called us in for lunch we were cold, red cheeked, wet, happy, hungry kids.

On days when the thermometer dropped below zero, we gathered round our new radio/record player. During the morning hours we listened to story records like 'Ber Rabbit', 'Bozo the Clown' and my favorite, 'So Dear to my Heart'. In the afternoon we tuned in our favorite radio programs. With the hot living room stove warming our backsides and our ears tuned to the static-laden radio, we joined the *Lone Ranger*, the *B Bar B Riders* or the *Royal Canadian Mounted Police* in fighting evildoers.

"I'm going out to get the clothes off the line. Behave yourselves while I'm gone," Mother would announce.

"Come with us now, to those thrilling days of yesteryear and the adventures of Sergeant Preston and his faithful dog, King!" the announcer shouted across the airwaves.

"Sure, Mom," we promised absentmindedly. "We'll be right here."

Engaged in an imaginary trek across the frozen north with King and Sergeant Preston, we didn't notice when, in a blast of cold air, Mother came through the backdoor with a basket full of frozen clothes. In the blink of an eye she was on us, icy fingers grabbing for each of us in turn. In mock terror we ran screaming through the house with her on our heels. Getting caught was half the fun as she snuggled her cold nose into our necks and thawed her frozen fingers on our warm backs.

Using our Christmas ice skates was not easy unless the summer rains had left some water behind in the reservoir. One winter when the reservoir was dry, I suggested to Mom that we skate in a frozen puddle that had formed in a low spot of the summer fallowed field across from the mail box.

"You can't skate in a field," Mom insisted. "It will ruin your skates."

I did not give up. The wide, ice puddle was just too inviting.

The argument continued. "Please, Mom, please," I begged.

Finally she gave in to my badgering. "Oh, for cry'n out loud! Go skate in the dirt, Little Miss Know–It–All."

"Aren't you going to give us a ride down?" I asked, pushing her apparent weakness to my advantage.

Rolling her eyes in exasperation, she buttoned us up, pulled our caps over our ears and threw our skates over our shoulders. "Out!" she ordered as she banged the door closed behind us.

"It's cold," Denny whined as we headed west.

"I don't like skating anyway," Butch complained as we sat on the frozen ground and pulled on our skates.

Bump, bump, bump we went over the furrowed field heading towards what looked like a smooth stretch of uninterrupted ice. As we stroked our skates across the frozen puddles and clumpy furrows we humped and bumped along, unable to gain any momentum.

Denny fell again and again, catching his skate blades on the dry spots which slowed my progress as I stopped to get him back on his feet. Moving on ahead, Butch yelled back that the ice was just as bad on the far end of the puddle.

"I want to go back," Denny bawled.

"This is no fun," Butch complained.

It was beginning to dawn on me that I might have made a mistake by insisting on this outing. My toes were turning numb inside my skates. The wind had come up, stinging my cheeks; my eyes started to water and my nose began to run.

"O.K. you big babies, we'll just go back," I yelled.

Without stopping to change into our boots we clomped back up the frozen road to the house in our ice skates.

"Good ice?" Mom inquired as she dried Denny's tears and unlaced his skates.

"Ya, but the boys are just big babies," I told her. "Just when it's getting fun they want to quit."

"Oh, that's too bad," she cooed with a wink in Butch's direction. Ignoring her tendency to gloat, I headed for the stove.

When the weather mandated indoor activities our living room stove was the focal point of life within the walls of our isolated ranch house. It stood against the far wall of our front room, and as the winds howled and the temperature dropped, we drew closer to its warmth. The card table was set up close by where we played the match game and solitaire or worked a puzzle. Our mittens steamed as they were laid out to dry on top of the stove. Cold, winter mornings would find us fighting for space by the stove as we dressed for the day.

"How much longer can I stay tucked under the covers?" I wondered, calculating the time I needed to jump from my bed so I could get to the stove before my brothers. "A few minutes longer," I promised myself as I savored the smell of perking coffee and listened for the sizzle of fresh side pork hitting Mom's frying pan.

Reluctantly, I decided it was time to make my move for the stove. Cautiously, so as not to wake the boys, I threw back my blankets, grabbed my school clothes, tiptoed past their beds and ran through the front room, plopping myself next to the glowing walls of the stove.

Wails filled the chilled air as the boys dragged themselves out of bed and demanded that I make room for them at the stove. Knowing that I had beaten them fair and square, I was determined to hold my ground.

"Scoot over," Dad ordered.

Protesting did little good with my father but I tried it anyway. "I was here first!" I insisted.

"Scoot!" he demanded with a firmness that led me to believe he meant business. So, fair or not, I moved over as the boys crowded tightly in around me. In a tangle of young legs and arms we pulled on jeans, shirts, socks and shoes generating enough body heat to overcome the cold surrounding the side of our frame turned away from the heat of the stove.

I didn't want to think about what came next but there was no avoiding our dash down the frosty, wooden walk to the outhouse. The first one dressed was usually the first one into the 'one hole'r' while the other two 'danced' around outside in the cold.

I was aware of the fact that other ranch homes in the valley had chamber pots tucked away under the bed of each sleeping room. Thinking that perhaps Mother had overlooked the possibility of chamber pots for our home, I casually suggested she consider getting some for our bedrooms.

"It will be a really cold day in you know where when I clean one of those filthy, stinking pee pots," she replied emphatically. I concluded that our desperate runs to the outhouse would continue.

After washing up in the kitchen sink and a hearty breakfast of pancakes and Zoom mush we bundled up for our ride to school. Dad, always concerned with our safety, took us to school during the winter months. He worried about the extreme cold and blizzards that could prove deadly for anyone caught out on the prairie without protection. Sometimes Dad found it necessary to string ropes from the house to the milking barn to make sure he could find his way back if a blizzard blew in unexpectedly. Wind-driven snow could erase the landscape in a matter of minutes, making it impossible to get one's bearings. During such whiteouts school would be cancelled and we drew even closer to the stove.

When I was in second grade the school furnace broke down. Linda's parents and mine discussed the situation over the phone and decided that we should have classes in the Meeks' home while Dad worked on the furnace. Our teacher, Miss Dahl, would stay with the Meeks family until the furnace was fixed and she could move back to the teacherage.

This was a welcome break in my winter routine but for Dad, fighting the drifts to get me the four miles to the Meeks place and then returning three miles back to the cold schoolhouse and working on the furnace all day, it must have been a real hardship.

Miss Dahl gathered her two pupils, Linda and I, around the kitchen table each morning for our lessons while Mrs. Meeks tried to keep Linda's little brothers quiet and away from our makeshift classroom. Midmorning we changed places as we broke for recess and a little bit of roughhousing with the boys in the living room while Mrs. Meeks started a pot of soup simmering on the back of the stove. At noon, Mr. Meeks arrived from the shop as books and lessons were cleared from the table, replaced with steaming bowls of soup and homemade bread and jam.

Dad came for me each day around mid afternoon. After filling up on coffee and bringing Bill up to date on the furnace repairs, he bundled me back in the pickup for the ride home. The road was easier to manage since Dad had now broken through the drifts coming and going. He relaxed behind the wheel and made an effort to engage me in conversation.

And it truly was an effort. While a great storyteller and a fellow who loved to socialize, Dad seemed uncomfortable conversing with his oldest daughter, unless of course, he was teasing or giving orders.

He began with the obvious. "So, how was school today?" he asked.

"Great!" I answered enthusiastically.

"Did you learn anything?" he wanted to know.

"Yep!" My conversation skills were limited as well.

By the time we reached the corner and turned east he had run out of questions and, because I didn't know how to inquire about furnace repairs, we traveled in silence, over the vast white landscape. The afternoon sun was moving westward, dropping behind the pickup, painting the fields and distant hills a luxurious pink and the sky beyond the windshield, a velvety purple. The air was cool and crisp, turning each breath we took into tiny patches of steam inside the truck. The only sound was the grinding of gears and the churning of the motor as Dad shifted into low to meet the challenge of an occasional frozen bank of snow drifting across the road.

I didn't need conversation. It was enough just to sit next to my Dad and have him all to myself for awhile. Between Grandpa, the boys, the hired men and, of course, Mother, Dad was nearly always occupied with someone or something. But for once, on those few days, coming and going from the Meeks' place, it was just the two of us, tightly bound in a common purpose and place. Dad, for that precious space of time, belonged only to me.

Eastern Montanans, caught in the dead of winter, fantasized about Chinooks which, in the blink of an eye, can turn bone chilling cold into spring like temperatures. Driven by a warm southwest wind, Chinooks dramatically change the landscape in a matter of a few hours. Drifts, taller than a third grader would be reduced to muddy puddles overnight. Thermometers, stuck at twenty below would soar to forty above in a single afternoon. Long time residents of the valley knew when a Chinook was coming. They could sense the change as the icy air took on a fresh smell, like sheets hung out to dry on a clothes line.

Scanning the sky, they watched it turn from a crisp, icy blue to a soft blue gray. Dry, powdery snow turned firm and compact under the farmer's boots. Soon, icicles were dripping from every overhang. Streams of water began trickling out from under snow banks as the corral and yard turned to a thick brown mud.

Children poured out of their houses unfettered by coats, caps and mittens. Housewives threw open windows and doors. It felt like spring! Sometimes that proved to be the case, but, more often than not, after a few days respite, winter roared back into the valley. No matter; a Chinook was God's promise that spring was on its way.

On the ranch, I learned to identify two sure signs of spring: daffodils and mud. I knew winter had run its course when, once each year, Mother brought home daffodils from the supermarket in Great Falls. Yellow as bright as sunshine, cheered us as she filled a vase with water and placed the bouquet in the middle of the kitchen table.

And the men around our table often needed cheering. If it had been a dry winter they were already worried about the income potential of their fall crops. If there had been a lot of winter snow they were fighting mud in the corrals, the roads and the fields. One year they fought to save our reservoir.

The coulees above the pasture had filled with snow the previous winter. In a normal year, this was a good thing, as the snow melted gradually, and by force of gravity, flowed gently downhill and seeped into the backside of the reservoir.

But this had not been a normal spring. Warm weather came quickly, followed by heavy and unrelenting rains, and with a rush; the snow tore down the gullies in torrents and poured into the reservoir. The high bank that Grandpa and Dad had built years before, across two low lying bumps in the landscape, was threatening to break loose. Neighbors arrived with tractors, teams and shovels, working beside Grandpa and Dad through the day and into the night.

Rocks piled at the lower end of Eloff's fields, were loaded on rock sleds and hauled to the reservoir wall where they were dumped against the back of the bank for added strength and support. A tumble bug worked the front of the bank sealing the break with dirt and rock. Leaks were plugged with gunny sacks and shovels. Taking turns from the backbreaking work, the men wandered into the kitchen for coffee and sandwiches served up by Mother throughout the night.

Regular bedtimes were forgotten as we waited anxiously, for each man's updated report.

"You better get some rest," Mom urged as she poured Dad a cup of coffee sometime after midnight.

"It's touch and go right now," Dad answered, downing his coffee and grabbing a sandwich as he headed out the backdoor. "We can't afford to take a break until we get the holes plugged."

I wondered if the house would be washed away. "What will happen if the dam breaks?" I asked nervously.

"Well, we won't have a reservoir anymore," Mom answered.

"Won't we be flooded out?" I was still a little worried. After all, we were directly downhill from the reservoir.

"No, but things will sure get muddy around here and your Grandpa and Dad will have to spend all summer rebuilding it. In the meantime, we'll have to pump water for the cattle all spring." She sounded tired.

By mid-afternoon of the second day, it looked like the reservoir was going to hold. Exhausted and mud covered, Grandpa and Dad thanked their neighbors and headed to the house for a nap. For weeks thereafter, they surveyed the dirt wall, watching for any wet spots that might indicate a weakening of the embankment. Eventually, the mud dried, sealing the dam like a cement glove.

The mud of Pleasant Valley was no ordinary mud. Montanans call it gumbo. Water and prairie soil, in the right combination, produces bumper crops of winter wheat. But when overly wet, it causes cattle, horses, pigs and ranchers to labor with every step as the gumbo fights to hang onto their weary legs. Pickups and cars, foolhardy enough to venture out on the roads after a soaking rain, would sooner or later find themselves waylaid by the gumbo. Slipping and sliding, rubber tires would lose traction and sink deep into the roadbed or glide awkwardly into a nearby ditch.

One spring Mother had managed to make it to town for much needed groceries but as we slid precariously down Chinaman Hill she voiced her concerns about getting back up the hill on our way home.

Approaching the dreaded incline later that afternoon we saw men, horses and vehicles up ahead. Usually quiet when Mom was negotiating bad roads, I wondered out loud, "What's going on up there?"

"It looks like they're pulling cars up the hill," Mom replied as she shifted into a lower gear and slowed the car. "This could get interesting," she muttered to no one but herself.

As we approached the hill one of the men slogged down to meet our green Chevy. Mother rolled down her window and listened intently as he explained the process.

Indicating the outfit ahead of us, he continued, "Soon as we get that fellow up on top, we'll be back for you, Jean. You stay behind the wheel and when you feel the horses start to pull, steer the car directly behind the team."

Surveying the car full of groceries and young bodies, he ordered us out of the car. "You kids get out and walk up. The less weight the better."

Grabbing Jimmy by the hand I followed Butch and Denny up the muddy incline. It was a warm spring day and by the time we reached the top of the hill we were sweaty and mud caked. The wind found us as we topped the coulee and turned to watch the action below.

Yelling men urged the team forward as harnesses and chains screeched and clanked. The horses strained against the load hitched behind them. With reins in hand, the teamster walked just behind his team encouraging them with steady, firm commands. Together, they slowly and deliberately, labored upwards. Just then the gumbo gave way and the pickup slid sideways, over the berm and towards the ditch.

"Whoa," the teamster shouted as he pulled back on the reins, halting the team. Men, standing to the side, rushed forward with shovels and began digging at the gumbo that had piled up around the pickup wheels.

"Giddy up," signaled the teamster as the sweating horses readied themselves for the last big pull that finally carried the truck up over the top of the hill. And then, it was Mom's turn.

Unhitching the team from the pickup, horses and driver headed back down the muddy slope to the bottom where Mother was waiting. I felt my body grow tense with worry. Butch and Denny, totally without concern, were energized by the action playing out before their eyes. In an effort to block the cold wind now blowing from the north, or maybe for reassurance, Jimmy pushed tightly up against me. I clung to his shoulders and held my breath.

All seemed to be going according to plan when, with a yank of the chains and a sickening swooshing sound, the Chevy slid sideways, over the bank, halting the horses in their muddy tracks.

Carefully and calmly the teamster adjusted the angle of the team. Several men raced to the back of Mother's vehicle and planted themselves against the trunk. As the teamster's "giddy up," encouraged the horses forward the men pushed from behind. Gradually the tires found solid ground and began, once again, to climb slowly towards the top of the coulee.

"Yea!" my brothers and I shouted as Mom, men and team crested the top of the hill.

With thanks and a wave to the men below, Mom ordered us into the car. Confidently she pointed our gumbo-laden vehicle towards home. There were still seven miles of ruts and mud to go but the worst was behind us. Supper would soon be on the table, spiced with tales of the day's exciting adventure.

Chapter 14 — Next Year

Weeks and months were measured by the change in our wheat crop. The brown and green of spring gradually turned into the dusky yellow of July. The hot, summer breezes of August dried the grain in its head, changing the fields, for miles in every direction, into a carpet of spun gold.

Dad and Grandpa closely monitored the crop's progress. Every rain, regardless of how scanty, was a major event followed by a trip to the rain gauges. Gauges, strategically nailed to the top of various fence posts in selected fields, measured the moisture a field received. The results were discussed at the kitchen table and later, if the fields were too wet to work, compared with other gauge readings across the county as farmers gathered in gas stations, hardware stores and bars.

"About an eighth of an inch on the Fox place; a little more up at the Wamsley place," Dad reported to Mother after an early morning survey of his rain gauges.

"Well, that's better than nothing," she'd offer as she flipped another pancake.

The crunch of the wheat kernels determined when the combines would roll into the fields. Following a practice that has been repeated by every grain grower from ancient Egypt until today, Dad waded out into the waving grain, snapped off a few heads, rubbed them between his palms, then opened his hands letting the wind blow away the chaff. Left behind were the kernels that would eventually, after being harvested and hauled to the elevator, become flour. For now, Dad placed a few kernels in his mouth and chewed thoughtfully, "Still pretty soft," meant that harvest was a few weeks off.

"Getting there," meant that the combine would be rolling into the fields by the end of the week.

Harvest was the high point of the year. Housewives loaded up on extra groceries knowing the days would be long and more men would be around the table at meal times. Kids helped out by shucking corn, drying dishes, swatting flies or just staying out of the way.

By now, a responsible farmer had his machinery in working order and a cadre of hired men waiting to go to work. If a good crop was at hand, a new grain truck or combine might be purchased on credit from the local implement dealer.

The first day of harvest began at seven or eight o'clock in the morning or just as soon as the morning breeze dried away the dew. As the hired men downed fried eggs and pancakes, Dad laid out the assigned tasks for the day. He would operate the new self-propelled combine and Grandpa would handle the fuel truck. That left shoveling and truck driving for the hired workers.

Starting the engine of the combine, Dad headed for the ripest field, followed by two grain trucks and Grandpa in the fuel truck. This was the moment of truth, the culmination of a year's labor. All the work, sweat and worry of the last year were on the line. All the hope, promise, even survival over the next twelve months, depended on this harvest.

Moving to the outside edge of the first strip in the field, Dad slowly engaged the lever, lowering the header down to ground level. Blades whirred as he approached the standing grain. As the header began to turn, the blades sliced the heads from their stalks and like magic, the big machine separated the kernels from the chaff, blowing straw out the back of the combine while carrying the grain up into the hopper behind the combine operator.

It usually took, depending on how many bushels the field was yielding, a few turns around the half mile strips, to fill the hopper. Next, the grain trucks moved alongside the combine; Dad lowered the auger and the grain cascaded down from the hopper into the truck bed like an avalanche of dusty copper pennies.

Climbing into the back of the truck, the hired man's job was to shovel the grain from the center of the truck bed to the far corners, distributing the load evenly. At first Dad came to a complete stop to unload but as he became more comfortable with the new machine and gained confidence in the truck driver, he began dumping on the go, while the truck moved alongside the combine, with the truck bed directly under the auger. Three or four dumps of the hopper filled the truck box and then, after securing a tarp over the load, the driver headed for the grain elevator twelve miles away in Fort Benton. Driver and truck number two then moved into position and the mechanical ballet began all over again.

It was a good harvest if this process could be controlled and synchronized throughout the next two weeks but all too often, the lines of grain trucks at the elevator would be long and slow moving. Sometimes a truck would break down as inexperienced drivers pushed the trucks too hard climbing up and over the hills and coulees on the way to town. And sometimes the hired man did not understand the urgency of the harvest and dawdled along the way. Experiencing Dad's anger and impatience usually convinced most of them to get on the ball or find another line of work.

Everyone, except the driver of the last truck filled, who had just left for town, would arrive in Mom's kitchen about midday for dinner. Butch and I were waiting on the back porch with warm water for the wash basin and Mom's old towels. As the men took their turn with soap and water, I stood by with the tea kettle, ready to refill the wash pan. When the water turned gray we slopped it into the yard or, if there was time, carefully carried it out front to pour on Mom's wilting flowers.

Convinced that working men needed food that would 'stick to their ribs', Mom prided herself on serving good food and lots of it. Taking their place at the kitchen table, the men filled up on fried chicken, roast beef or maybe pork chops. There might be mashed potatoes or fresh dug new potatoes and lots of garden vegetables. If sliced, fresh tomatoes were on the menu, Dad and Grandpa revived their ongoing debate. Grandpa liked sugar sprinkled on his tomatoes. Dad ate his plain. Mother basked in the admiration of the hired men as they voiced their appreciation for her fresh baked cakes and pies that completed every midday meal served during harvest.

Thrilled with new faces around our kitchen table and having never taken our Grandmother's admonition that 'children should be seen and not heard' too seriously, my brothers and me filled the lunch hour with one story after another. Wrapping up what we thought was an especially exciting tale, Grandpa would add, "and the next day it rained."

Trying to outwit his fatalistic ending, we rambled on and on, hoping that just once he might forget his line. Then, just as we ran out of breath or out of story, Grandpa, with perfect timing, announced "and the next day it rained." The hired men, who were not acquainted with this routine, rocked with laughter. Mother, who had heard the game one time too many, rolled her eyes while Dad reminded us that we should be quiet and clean our plates.

The first truck driver usually arrived just as the rest of us were finishing the meal. While he washed up and filled his plate, the second loaded truck headed for town. Grandpa returned to the field, ahead of the crew, to gas up and grease the combine, while Dad took a few minutes to fill Mom in on the strategy for the afternoon. She needed to know which field they would move to next, what time she should bring out a lunch and how many she should expect for supper. And "Oh, did you call Great Falls about that part we need by tomorrow. See if they will send it down on the bus so we can have it by morning," he called over his shoulder as the screen door slammed shut behind him.

Hot was synonymous with harvest. It would be the hottest part of the afternoon when Mom pulled into the field with the men's lunch. While we waited at the end of the strip for the combine to come around, Mother opened her car door and instructed me to do the same. Like magic, the blistering summer wind was transformed into a cool breeze as it blew through one open door and out the other. Tired, dusty men gathered around and under the vehicles, anywhere they might capture a little shade, while Mom and I passed out sandwiches, cookies and coffee.

Before we left, the crew brought their water bags to be refilled with the fresh, cool water we had brought from the house. Every vehicle and the combine carried a canvas bag designed to hold drinking water. Hanging the bag on the shady side of the truck kept the water cool most of the morning but in the afternoon, when the sun was hot and the wind, blistering, the water turned warm and tasteless.

Supper would be served late into the evening since the combine rolled as long as the wheat stayed dry enough to cut. Once the dew returned, toughening the grain, men and machinery pulled out of the fields. Grandpa headed for town where Grandma would have his supper waiting. Nearly too tired to eat, the hired men cleaned up at the kitchen sink, downed a light supper and headed for the bunkhouse. Dad went out to take care of any last minute barnyard chores while Mom cleaned up the kitchen and began thinking about breakfast.

Tired, but satisfied with the day's accomplishments, and alone for the first time that day, we relaxed for a few minutes before climbing into bed. A cool breeze, carrying cricket music with it, blew through the open kitchen windows.

"How do crickets make that sound?" I asked my exhausted father.

Too tired for a detailed explanation, even if he knew one, Dad told me that they sang by rubbing their legs together and the louder their song, the more likely it was that it would rain. I went to bed, listening and hoping that the cricket's song would not get too loud, at least until harvest was over.

Most summer evenings brought very little relief from the heat. The kitchen light continued to burn as Mom and Dad waited for their bedroom, which faced west, to cool off. The hired men sat outside on the bunkhouse steps where they could catch an occasional breeze. If it was unusually hot, Mother would let Butch and me sleep in the double bed at the far end of the back porch. Screens kept the mosquitoes out but let the glow of the hired men's cigarettes and their conversations filter through. I strained to hear every word. However, as Butch drifted off and my pillow heated up, I forgot to listen, focusing instead on my sweating curls and the cool underside of my pillow. Turning it over and back again, I waited for the voices to cease and the light in the kitchen to go off. Eventually the night air cooled and without knowing it, I gave way to the luxurious sort of sleep that only comes after a long, busy day.

Sleep was always in short supply during harvest time. Late nights, early mornings and hard, long days turned our joy and excitement into drudgery and stress as we entered our second week of harvest.

"Did that combine part come?" "What in the hell is that truck driver doing in town?" "If you'd stop napping in the truck, you'd be here when I need you!" Grandpa and Dad were becoming testy with each other and short tempered with the hired men. Mother was growing weary since she was the first one up to fix breakfast and usually the last one down at night. Open warfare was declared on kids who were no longer interested in doing their share but now devoted their time to horseplay and getting under foot.

"Jean, do you want one of those kids to get killed?" Dad demanded of my worn out Mother. Always fearful that a truck might back over a child too small to be seen in a rearview mirror, Dad was furious when he found us playing in and around the parked grain trucks as the hired men finished their noon meal.

Dad rephrased his concern. "Someone's going to back over one of those kids if you don't keep them up around the house when the trucks are in the yard."

"Well, I can't do everything around here," she snapped as Dad stalked out, slamming the screen door behind him.

We tried to do better. We set the table; we swatted more flies, gathered the eggs and stayed away from the trucks. During supper we kept our mouths shut and our eyes on our plates. Hugs and apologies put us all to bed with a sense that tomorrow would be a better day. We were beginning to understand the importance of these few intense weeks to our family unit and we were learning that it was hard, tough work. We were learning to be part of a team.

And losing, for our team, was not an option. Our livelihood depended on at least breaking even. That meant bills could be paid off at the grocery store, the feed store, the fuel bill and most importantly, the loan at the P.C.A. A full payoff assured the issuance of a new loan to keep us going until next year's crop came through. The new loan assured the farmer that he could operate and keep his family fed and clothed until the next harvest. Paying your bills was crucial to maintaining a line of credit with local merchants.

"Next year," was a promise we made to ourselves. A promise that we would work hard, that we would guard what little resources we had and that we would not get discouraged. "Next year," was also a hope. A hope that the weather would cooperate, that the money would not run out and that God would reward honest effort.

If the yield had been above average and the grain prices reasonable; if Dad had managed to outwit the insects, avoid the hail and outsmart the weather man, we could truly call it a 'good year'. A good year meant extra money for new farm equipment, new furniture or maybe, if it was a 'really good year', a new car.

It also meant trips to Great Falls for school clothes. The summer work had turned Mother into a fine-tuned machine, capable of going up one side of Central Avenue and down the other for hours on end. For her, shopping was serious business. She knew what she was after and she didn't quit until she got it, ran out of money or the stores closed, whichever came first.

"They have to push her out to lock the doors at night," Dad joked.

Dad's job was to wait patiently in the Johnson Hotel and keep an eye on us kids. The hotel lobby was lined with leather couches and chairs which were occupied by other farmers doing the same job for their wives. Talk of cattle prices, politics and the weather filled the stale, smoke-filled lobby while the younger kids played amongst the furniture, crawling over their fathers' laps and peeking into the packages that had begun to pile up around the farmers' feet. As the day progressed the wives returned for lunch, for another child that needed to try on a coat she had found on sale at the J.C. Penny store or for additional cash from their husbands' wallet.

It was hard to keep track of the older kids. They streamed out on to Central Avenue, shopping with their summer wages, sharing a coke at the dime store with other teenagers or maybe shoplifting a few nonessential items out from under the noses of clerks too busy to notice.

My brothers headed for the local western store. The clerks and saddle makers didn't seem to mind as the boys tried out every saddle in the back room of Arios. Their next stop was an imaginary ride on the motorcycles at the Sears Farm Store. Following Dad's orders to check in periodically, they'd reluctantly abandon their fantasies and wander back to the hotel, where they joined me and other farm kids at the comic book counter in the far corner of the hotel lobby.

Regardless of how many comic books we might read there on the marble floor of the hotel we always spent a few dimes to take our favorites home. I guess the hotel allowed the practice, knowing that they would sell comics and that we would do less damage to their establishment if we were reading instead of chasing each other around the lobby.

If my grandparents were also in Great Falls, we'd meet for lunch at Grandma's favorite place, The Cafeteria. As tantalizing smells drifted down the sidewalk, long lines of hungry families began to form at the door around the noon hour. Since Dad was stationed at the Johnson Hotel, just next door, it was his job to get a spot in line. Dad hated standing in line, especially if he had two or three kids in tow. Working our way through the doors we were greeted by steam tables laden with roast beef, ham, and chicken; trays of corn, green beans and mashed potatoes. Encouraged by our grandparents to help ourselves to whatever caught our fancy, we loaded up on extra helpings of jello blocks, custard and maybe even, pie. Mom protested that we should choose just one, but pretending not to hear, Grandma pushed us along to the drink section. Grandmother and I were usually the first ones through the line and it was our job to find a table big enough for all of us. Dad brought up the rear, still grumbling about the crowds, the noise and the lines.

After lunch we gathered outside on the sidewalk so that the adults could discuss and decide on the afternoon activities. Mother's list always dictated the schedule.

"Can we go to the matinee? Please, please!" we begged bouncing up and down on the sidewalk as they tried to talk over our pleadings.

If Mother didn't need us to try something on or if Dad was feeling generous they usually said yes, relieved to have us off the streets while they finished up their errands.

Dad and Grandpa would return to the hotel lobby or maybe take the little ones and drive out to the edge of town, through the back lots of implement dealerships, checking out new and used equipment. After getting us off to the Liberty Theater, Mom and Grandma were free to shop at a more leisurely pace, checking out a new hat or some beautiful, but unnecessary household item.

The Liberty Theater was a glamorous place. A chandelier hung overhead; rich red carpet ran the length of the lobby and up the long, graceful, gold encrusted ramps, which wound their way to the marbled bathrooms and balcony on the second floor.

Handing over our quarters for the movie and our dimes for popcorn, Butch, Denny and I entered the fantasy world of Lassie, Roy Rogers and Dale Evans or Black Beauty.

Too soon, we were blinking back the late afternoon sunlight as we exited the theater, looking for our ride back to the real world. Sometimes we found our grandparents waiting for us in their shiny maroon Packard. All the way home, they patiently listened to our retelling of the movie plot and our pleadings to return next week so we could see part seven of the serial '*Adventures of Flash Gordon*'. The hour long ride gave our grandparents time to relate stories about the 'olden days', hints about what Mom had bought for us and maybe even, if they were lucky, naps for their grandchildren. Great Falls was a great place!

The start of school and the last of the garden signaled the end of summer. After the last few tough ears of corn had been eaten and the last quart of beans had been canned it was time to dig the potatoes. This big job was usually directed by my Grandfather. Dad was not in favor of having a garden. He thought it was too much work for Mom and, besides, most vegetables could now be bought in cans at the grocery store. But with summer chores winding down there were few excuses left and so the whole family found themselves in the garden surrounded by dead potato vines.

Turning over the piles of dirt underneath the vines, we found the potatoes, camouflaged like soldiers outfitted for desert warfare. Brown skinned potatoes, caked with gumbo, lay hidden in the ground waiting for searching fingers and pitch forks to turn them over and raise them up into the light of day.

Once the potatoes were on top of the ground every available youngster was recruited to pick them up and throw them into gunnysacks. The work began for us older ones when we arrived home from school. The lingering heat of summer caused us to sweat as we dragged our gunnysacks along behind us, picking up the waiting potatoes, row after row.

The short summer day soon turned into a crisp fall evening. As the sun moved west, Grandpa set a match to the dry corn stocks piled up at the far end of the garden. The fire crackled as smoke and flames soared into an orange and purple sky, inviting us to warm our stiff, cold fingers and dirt encrusted knees. Later, Grandma and Mom returned from the house with hot dogs and buns for our supper meal while Dad cut each of us a green stick from the shelter belt and trimmed it to a sharp point.

Creeping ever closer to the fire we extended our stick and hot dog out over the flames turning our faces away from the searing heat.

"Put it there, under the fire, down by the coals," Grandma directed.

Soon we each had found our own little oven amongst the glowing coals. Methodically turning our wiener and stick we watched as the meat began to brown, then swell and finally crack open, letting the steaming fat sizzle its way into the flames.

"Perfect!" we announced as we tucked the hot, blackened meat into a waiting bun.

Tomorrow Dad and Grandpa would come through with the pickup, load the lumpy gunnysacks scattered throughout the garden and haul them to the root cellar. It was comforting to know that thousands of potatoes would be available all winter long, waiting to be turned into fried potatoes on a Friday night, potato soup on a cold blustery winter day or, maybe, if Mother was so inclined, lefsa for a Christmas treat.

But tonight would be our last evening together in the night air. We lingered while the glowing coals turned to gray, dying embers before heading up to the house. Linking arms and holding hands, we carried the warmth of the fire all the way back to the house.

With only a child's understanding, I failed to grasp the importance of all the family had accomplished over the last few months but I was old enough to know that the grown-ups were pleased with us and with themselves. Working together, we had managed to produce the resources our two families needed to carry us through the upcoming winter and on into spring. And like the back breaking, tedious job we had just completed, we had shared some fun along the way.

Secure and protected in the confines of our family circle, I ran on ahead, into the dark towards the yard light. I could not imagine that evenings such as these would be coming to an end and that the events and circumstances of "next year" would drag us all into the darkness of family discord and finally, separation.

Chapter 15 — Red Letter Days

"Just knock on the door and run back here," Mom instructed Butch and me in a hoarse whisper.

I wasn't sure about any of this. Even though I was very young I knew my Grandmother would not appreciate a trick played on her and besides that, using the front door of her house was forbidden, at least for the grandkids.

But, as instructed, we knocked and then ran to the outside of the hedge where Grandmother's front walk joined the town sidewalk and where Mother was waiting, crouched and still.

"You didn't knock loud enough," Mom said as she sent us back up the sidewalk. Once again, Butch and I knocked on the door and ran back to our hiding place.

It was a beautiful May day, the first to be exact. Grandma's tulips were in full bloom; the lilacs were in the process of forming plump little purple buds while gigantic cottonwoods glistened overhead with new, green leaves glowing in the late afternoon sun.

Mother, Butch and I had worked through the morning folding doilies into funnel shapes, attaching fuzzy pipe cleaner handles with glue and then filling our creations with little candies and cookies that Mother had made the day before. We'd even gone out into the new grass and picked a few fuzzy, yellow dandelions and tucked them in around the goodies.

Mystified with the process, but caught up in Mother's celebratory mood, we packed our lacey bundles into an old shoe box and headed for town. There was one each for our Grandparents and another couple for Aunt Dawn and Uncle Pierre and, even though we were not regular attendees, a couple for our minister and his wife.

At long last, the big wooden door opened. Grandma growled her displeasure at finding her front stoop deserted, followed by squeals of pleasure, and what I'm fairly certain was mock surprise, at finding our May baskets propped up on her doorstep.

"Happy May Day!" we yelled as we jumped from our hiding place and ran up the walk. Grandma was so pleased that she forgot her rule and invited us in, right through the front door.

Gradually, with each passing season, I was learning that, while most days were about waking, working and sleeping, there were special days, usually marked in red on Dad's Farmer's Elevator calendar. While cows still had to be milked and livestock fed, these interludes were like post-it notes on an office 'to do' bulletin board, reminding everyone that some fun should be scheduled into every season.

As I grew older, I began to notice that these special occasions could bring my world to a complete stop, at least for awhile, throwing adults, children, extended family and even the store owners in town, into an alternate universe of goodwill and good times.

My Grandmother was the driving force behind our holiday celebrations. She provided the space, the good china and the main course. My aunts and Mother were expected to arrive with side dishes and desserts as well as clean, well behaved children.

I suspected that fathers and grandfathers were not all that crazy about these special occasions but tolerated them only because they knew holiday gatherings were important to the women. And, of course, lounging around with the other men folk and eating fine food was an added incentive for the short term abandonment of field and chores.

Truth be told, the women probably cleaned and cooked and shopped and cooked some more, wrapped gifts, planned activities, and wore themselves out cleaning up after everyone, not because they loved doing it, but for the benefit of their youngsters.

For us kids, it was a day of fun with our cousins, teasing from our uncles and plates piled high with fruit salad. While vaguely aware that our mother and grandmother appeared frazzled and at times, exhausted, none of us, at that young age, were wise enough to grasp the wonderful truth that they were creating for us, out there in the steamy kitchen, a heritage of holiday memories and family traditions.

Thanksgiving was just such a time.

Across the river and through the coulees to our cousin's grandparent's home we'd go! It was at least a thirty mile drive which took, because of the rough gravel roads, nearly an hour.

Without seatbelts we were free to push and shove our way around the back seat in order to gain a better view of the scenery or poke our heads out the window to avoid Dad's cigarette smoke.

It might have had something to do with wear and tear on the brake pads but once behind the wheel, Dad did not believe in stopping no matter how desperate things got in the back seat. Blood could be oozing out on to the running boards but he kept the car moving forward. Threats and warnings would have to suffice, at least until we arrived at our eventual destination.

"Jean, settle those kids down back there," he'd shout over the roar of the engine and the squalls coming from the backseat.

Half turning in her seat she'd separate the quarreling factions and establish some sort of order, but on this particular Thanksgiving trip to the Peres farm Mother already had her hands full with three pumpkin pies.

One pie had been placed cautiously on the car floor boards between her shoes and the other two were balanced precariously on her lap.

In order to accommodate the pies, Jimmy, who usually rode in front, between my parents, had been placed in the back seat next to me.

Maybe it was the crowded conditions or maybe just too much sugar on their breakfast Rice Krispies that triggered my brother's backseat bickering. Whatever the cause, even I knew that my quarrelling brothers were pushing Dad's patience to the breaking point.

As we crossed the bridge leading southwest out of Fort Benton and up on to the Highwood bench, the fighting escaladed. Mom, with a pie in each hand, was totally neutralized and restricted to yelling over her shoulder. Over estimating my ability to settle my brothers down, she ordered me to intervene. This only served to aggravate the situation.

Dad increased the pressure on the accelerator calculating that the faster he went, the sooner we would arrive and he could administer the paddling he was sure we deserved. Meantime, he was limited to reinforcing

Mother's threats with a few of his own and reaching over the front seat to pinch or relocate whichever one of his sons was within range of his long right arm.

Suddenly, a terrible and sickening quiet descended upon the occupants of our overloaded sedan. Slipping and sliding in the icy gravel, Dad, unable to navigate a wide right angle turn, sent us careening across the road and into the ditch.

Mom's pies were strewn upside down across the front seat, most coming to rest in Dad's lap. Our car was nose down over the side of the gravel road, window deep in brown crusty weeds still tipped with morning frost. Somehow I just knew this was going to ruin our Thanksgiving.

Forcing the driver's door open, Dad pulled himself out of the car and scraped the pie residue off his one good pair of dress slacks. His quiet, controlled demeanor only served to further terrorize the four of us as we unscrambled ourselves in the back seat. One by one he dragged us out of the car. The sound of three good whacks, one for each of his male offspring, cracked like broken glass across the empty prairie.

"Go help your Mother," he ordered me as he inspected the damage and slope of the ditch.

Her door was already open as Mother struggled to climb up and out of the front seat. I grabbed her outstretched pumpkin stained hand, planted my feet firmly in the gravel and pulled her out on to the road where she immediately busied herself scraping the pumpkin off her shoes.

We were a sorry looking bunch, standing out there on the windswept plains of Chouteau County, shivering and subdued as Dad tried to maneuver the Chevrolet out of the ditch. Dirt, mixed with a skiff of snow, flew as the wheels churned on the icy weeds. Eventually the tires gained enough traction to pull our car back onto the road.

"Get in," Dad commanded. We didn't need to be told twice. We finished the trip in total silence, hardly able to imagine the punishment and humiliation that awaited us upon arrival.

By the time we pulled into the Peres' yard, Dad had cooled off considerably and was already beginning to frame the episode into a story, embellishing it and searching for laugh lines. The doomsday scenario that we had been contemplating was beginning to dissipate.

His audience; aunts, uncles, grandparents and cousins winked and giggled as Dad spun his tale between servings of turkey, dressing and candied sweet potatoes. Instead of the disobedient little brats we had imagined ourselves to be, Dad related the story in such a way that his children were just overly rambunctious, lovable little goof-offs.

We had a lot to be thankful for that Thanksgiving but I was especially grateful for our Dad's good humor and storytelling skills, which had not only saved the holiday, but had transformed a calamity into a fun-filled comedy with his kids as the star performers. Mother did not, however, join in the laughter. As I stifled giggles behind my napkin, I sensed that she was still a little peeved. In her book, there was nothing funny about bad behavior and at this point in time, it was her husband's behavior that she thought needed correcting.

"Bill, you are just encouraging them to behave like little barbarians when you go on like that," she said with a glare in his direction.

With a wink and a grin, Dad conceded her point. "You're right Jean. And just to teach them a lesson; they can't have any pumpkin pie for dessert." Finally, Mother laughed along with the rest of us.

Memorial Day was an important undertaking in our family and town. Back then it was referred to as 'Decoration Day' because, as Grandma explained it, "we decorate the graves." The activities began the day before with an inventory.

"Do you have any tulips left?" Grandma would inquire of Mother and Aunt Dawn. Out in the country, beyond a reliable water source, Grandma's daughters never had an overabundance of any type of blooms but on Decoration Day flowers were an absolute necessity.

"Only a few but I've got some iris just opening up." Mother would offer.

"Well, bring what you've got and don't forget to bring some empty coffee cans." Already, Grandma was matching, in her head, the number of graves she was responsible for, the lilacs, tulips and iris available and the amount of tinfoil she would need to turn coffee tins into vases.

The morning of Decoration Day was spent filling buckets with water and cut flowers as the men loaded them, the cans, spades and garden tools into waiting car trunks and pickup beds.

With our initial tasks completed we took a break to watch the parade just beginning to form on Front Street. Grandpa walked with us as far as the corner of the Pioneer but my brothers and I were eager to be nearer the bridge so we could watch the color guard throw the memorial wreath in the river.

The parade consisted of a few floats, at least one of which was usually topped off with fake gravestones and lilies, all perched on the flat bed of a grain truck. The County Commissioners and Mayor, interspersed among the floats, bounced along in antique cars. The Sheriff's Posse, twenty or thirty strong, mounted on horses of every color and size, added to the excitement. At the front of the parade, a mismatched cadre of old soldiers, dressed in pea green wool, represented their war; World War I. The men of World War II followed in their airmen, sailor and infantry uniforms, most of which were too tight and bulged at the buttons. They carried the flags proudly and stepped in unison to the beat of the high school band, following directly behind the old soldiers.

The procession stopped twice, first at the memorial to the county's World War I dead, which was stationed in the middle of Front Street across from the Grand Union. A wreath was laid respectfully and a salute given. The next stop was a block further along at the intersection to the bridge.

It wasn't easy to get a choice spot next to the bridge. It seemed everyone in the county wanted to be in the same place. Pushing and shoving, we worked our way to the front of the crowd.

"You boys get your hats off," a bystander growled at my brothers. All around us kids were being jerked to attention; their caps pulled off and ordered to put their hand over their heart.

"Haven't you learned a thing in school? The right hand! Like this!"

"Were they talking to me?" I wondered. Quickly I straightened my back and found my heart just as the rifles cracked out their salute. A lone trumpeter's melancholy strains of 'Taps' echoed off the hills along the river as the wreath landed in the Missouri with a splash.

As the color guard took their positions back on the street, the band played something patriotic while nervous horses danced and whinnied, anxious to be moving once again. Finally, as one, the entire parade began moving along the street towards the park where they eventually disbanded.

Returning to Grandma's house, we found the women ready to leave for the graveyard. We had our choice; stay behind with the men or play amongst the tombstones. The tombstones always won.

Carefully, so as not to spill the water buckets in the trunk, we climbed the first set of hills above town, crossed the railroad tracks, and continued up the hill, past the Shep monument, and on to the stone gateway of the graveyard. Intentional or just a lovely accident, the gate framed a perfect likeness of the Madonna formed by the ever present snow on Mt. Baldy, clearly visible, twenty miles to the south.

We were in a hurry. Every year we raced to the steep cliff, high above the river, to see if we could spot the wreath that had been thrown into the river less than an hour ago.

"There it is!" I yelled, finger pointed downward towards a wide bend in the river.

My eyesight was faulty. "That's just a log or something," Butch informed me. "I think we missed it."

"We always miss it." Denny was in the habit of calling a spade a spade.

He was right. We were always behind or ahead of the river's flow. I wished I knew which.

Grandma, Mother and Aunt Dawn busied themselves pulling prairie grass from the grave sites, sloshing water into coffee cans and filling them with flowers. As we helped place the bouquets on the individual graves Grandma would remind us of the life of the departed, who they were related to and how they had died.

"What an improvement," Aunt Dawn observed as she stretched her back and admired their morning's handiwork.

"The flowers won't last the day up here in the sun and wind," Mom chimed in. She, like her son Denny, was a realist.

Grandma was ready to go. "Well, we did our best. Let's go get some lunch."

The most difficult phase of Decoration Day was yet to come. After lunch and bidding Aunt Dawn, Uncle Pierre and Vicky goodbye, the rest of us cleaned up and piled into two cars for the trip to the mausoleum in Great Falls.

The mausoleum was not like the graveyard where running and shouting, while discouraged, was permissible. The building was a labyrinth of marbled corridors, high ceilings and stained glass. Organ music played quietly in the background. Any exploring done in these hallowed halls, had to be done on tiptoe and in whispers.

But the restrained, quiet decorum of the sanctuary did not dampen my brother's curiosity. Every year Grandpa was barraged by the same, predictable questions.

"Yes, there are dead people behind every one of the places where you see a nameplate," he answered patiently, his voice several decibels lower than usual. We busied ourselves counting the tombs without nameplates and found that there was room for a lot more dead people in our wing of the building.

"How do they get the dead people in there?" Jimmy wanted to know.

"They pull the crypt out and put the body in, shut it up tight and seal it," Grandpa responded in a half whisper.

"No, I don't think they can get the body out again." It seemed to me that Grandpa's voice had raised an octave or so.

"I can't believe how stupid the boys are," I thought to myself, with eyes rolled ceiling ward, forgetting that I had asked similar questions in the not-too-distant past.

With an edge to his voice, Grandpa fielded the next question. "Well, I suppose, if the family really wanted to move the body or something. I don't know. And that's enough questions. Just be quiet for awhile."

I could tell that Grandpa was losing patience and that a walk to the car, inquisitors in tow, might be coming next.

But the questions continued. "Yes, your Grandmother and I will be buried here when we die. In those two; right below your sister's," he quipped, indicating two crypts, both without nameplates.

Exasperation was beginning to set in. "I don't know when!"

I thought that maybe his voice was getting a little too loud for the mausoleum. But my brothers were not done asking questions.

"Because your Grandmother doesn't want to be buried in dirt, that's why! Now, for the last time, pipe down!"

"Roy, shss!" Grandma warned with a glare in his direction.

Even the boys finally realized that the discussion was now closed.

Mother and Grandma had just returned from somewhere in the depths of the building where water and a special bouquet they had ordered from The Electric City Conservatory were placed in a vase. A respectful, neatly dressed attendant, who never spoke above a whisper, placed the vase, now filled with our fresh flowers, into a bracket at the end of a long pole, and lifted it high up to the top tier without spilling a drop. Carefully, he transferred it to the bracket on the front of Lana's crypt, right next to her nameplate.

For a short while, our parents and grandparents stood in silence, each arm in arm. Tears quietly traced a path down the contours of my Mother's and Grandmother's upturned faces. It was then that my brothers and I, sensitive to what they were experiencing and having some small heartaches of our own, finally turned solemn and attentive. And then, with a dab of a crisp, white hanky, a turn toward the hall and a soft grip of the hand, we were quietly ushered out into the sunshine. Decoration Day was over for another year.

Contrary to popular assumptions; sentimentality and religious conviction does not drive the average child's vision of Christmas. At least it didn't at our house. Since we hardly ever went to church we did not connect the holiday with the baby Jesus or his birthday. And since we were not Catholic, there were no strolls to

Midnight Mass in the moonlight with snowflakes falling softly on our eyelashes. And finally, since we were not a musical family there was no singing of Christmas carols around Grandma's beautiful upright piano which sat, continually silent, against the wall of her parlor, along with the brocaded chairs we were not allowed to sit on. For us; my brothers and me, Christmas, plain and simple, was about Santa Claus and getting stuff.

When we were small and Grandma and Grandpa had not yet started spending their winters in Arizona, our gifts were hauled out from under our Christmas tree at the ranch, to their house in town.

I don't know how many trips Dad made to and from the car but I do remember his complaints as the gift wrapped packages were transferred from our car trunk to Grandma's front room, spilling around her tree and piling up in the corners.

Dad's complaints were predictable. "I've never seen anything so ridiculous. First we haul all this stuff from the stores to home then we pack it all up again and bring it back to town. And after it's all over, I load it up again and drag it back to the ranch. Now Jean, does that make one bit of sense to you?"

"Oh, don't be such a grouch! It's Christmas!" Mother was in high spirits and she would not let Dad's wet blanket spoil her favorite holiday.

I didn't understand Dad's objection to our excessive Christmas celebrations until I was much older. It wasn't just about too many gifts and packing them up and down my grandparent's sidewalk. As a child of the depression and a broken home Dad was opposed, always, to any show of pretentiousness or self-indulgence. He didn't indulge himself and he didn't believe in indulging his children. Lucky for us, Mom had no such inhibitions.

There were ice skates, toy trucks, gun holsters, books, wood burning kits, puzzles, erector sets and Lincoln Logs and best of all, no clothes. And even though we were not at our house, Santa seemed to know where we were on Christmas Eve and stopped there first, on his way to Christmas morning.

Someone, usually an adult, would be the first to hear the sleigh bells jingling or the reindeer hooves click, clacking on the patio. The next thing we knew there was a loud knock at the front door and a rousing "Ho! Ho! Ho!" But no matter how fast we raced through the piles of boxes and tangles of wrapping paper we could not get to the door fast enough to catch a glimpse of the old fellow. Disappointment faded fast, however, when we spotted the two story dollhouse and Red Rider rifles that Santa left behind, just for us.

Total happiness has a way of wearing a child out. The thrill of our new playthings began to wane at about the same time we downed the last of Grandma's sugar cookies. Mother finished sorting the gifts from the wrappings while Dad completed his final round trip to the car trunk. Dazed, but contented, Butch, Denny and I crunched along the snowy path, following our parents to the waiting car. A warm stream of air flowed from the heater and into the back seat where, without quarreling, we found our own space and snuggled down into our sheep skin coats and caps for the ride home. All three of us were asleep before Dad pulled up out of the river bottom.

Tomorrow, around midday, we'd be back for ham, scalloped potatoes, pecan pie, red punch, Mother's famous plum pudding and Canasta.

Like it or not, Canasta was mandatory at all Grandma's holiday gatherings. The dining room table was cleared and the cards pulled out of the top drawer of the buffet along with Grandma's hand cranked shuffle machine that someone had given her on a prior Christmas Eve.

Six handed Canasta, with three decks, is not a kids' game so finding a lap or pulling a chair up beside an adult was as close as we got to the action, which lasted, sometimes, until early evening. Once the winning team was finally declared, the food came out again.

As the bananas in the fruit salad turned a mushy brown and the last of the dinner rolls were warmed in paper sacks in the oven, quiet conversation gradually replaced the exuberance of the holiday season. Christmas seemed to be in the process of being wrapped in memory paper, placed on the top shelf of a distant closet, waiting until next year, to be pulled down and opened once again.

Our Christmas celebrations changed dramatically after our grandparents took out a small homestead in Arizona. Thereafter, each October, the family gathered to help load their car from stem to stern with bulging suitcases and a dozen or so of Grandma's hat and shoe boxes. Eventually there were the final hugs, kisses and tears as we stood on the curb waving them goodbye.

To compensate for the winter loss of our Grandparents, Mother started taking us to Sunday School. It was there that we finally started to learn about the importance of Jesus' birthday and the words to the Christmas carols. We also had parts to learn for the Christmas program.

Mother, always the teacher, drilled us incessantly.

"Now, repeat after me," she ordered. "Fear not, for behold, I bring you good tidings of great joy, which shall be to all people!" she exclaimed with unbounded enthusiasm and confidence.

"Fear not," I began hesitatingly. "For I have good news of joy...." My voice faded along with my memory into 'I can't land'.

"Kareen, we've been over this a half dozen times. You have to get this pretty soon. The program is Sunday night. And put some enthusiasm into it! Remember, you've got good news!"

About the same time I started learning about Jesus I began to have my doubts about Santa Claus.

"You know, there isn't any Santa Claus," Roger announced one day as we gathered up our lunch boxes from the school cloak room.

"There is so," Denny protested.

Roger was emphatic. "I'm not joking. Santa is not real. Grown-ups just make up all that Christmas stuff."

I wanted to hear more. "How do you know?" I challenged him.

"I just know," he responded as he dipped a drink out of the water bucket before heading back into the classroom.

I was left with my doubts. Come to think of it, that fellow we had our picture taken with at the department store didn't have a real beard and I was pretty sure there was a pillow under his red suit. Mother had explained that he was one of Santa's helpers. But maybe it was all a ruse. Maybe the grown-ups were trying to fool us.

Well, Christmas was just around the corner and I promised myself that one way or another, this year, I was going to find out if Santa Claus was real or just another adult snow job.

The day before Christmas we were on our way to town for some last minute shopping. Mother needed a few things for our Christmas dinner and we, with dimes, nickels and maybe even a shiny silver dollar jingling in our pocket, needed to shop for our Mother's gift. Dad escorted us from store to store as the three of us endeavored to select the perfect gift for our Mother.

A shiny broach at the back of the drug store's jewelry cabinet caught my eye. "How much is that one?" I asked.

"Four ninety-nine," the clerk responded patiently.

"You don't have that much," Dad reminded me. Always in a hurry when shopping for anything except machinery, he was growing weary of my indecisiveness.

"How about that one?" I asked pointing to a smaller version of the first.

"We'll take it," Dad interjected. Since I was still a few coins short he made up the difference from his own pocket of change.

Along with Dad, Butch and Denny were also anxious to put an end to my Christmas shopping. Early on the boys had pooled their funds and purchased a cup and saucer for Mom's teacup collection.

Shopping finally completed, we headed for a local café to meet Mother for our evening meal.

"Let's go home for supper," the boys pleaded. The long wait, to get to their gifts under our Christmas tree, was making them edgy.

"Your Mom's worked hard and deserves a night out," Dad insisted as we slid into the big corner booth near the back of the restaurant.

"But what if Santa comes and we're not there?" Butch wanted to know. Obviously, he had not taken Roger's revelation too seriously.

Mom took her own sweet time finishing her meal. "Oh, I don't think he'll come before we get there," she said as she dawdled over her lemon pie.

Now it was my turn to get impatient. All this talk about Santa and him knowing where we were and what we wanted and how we behaved was beginning to wear a little thin.

"The boys are falling for all this Santa Claus stuff," I remember thinking. "But I'm beginning to have my doubts."

"I'm ready," I announced, eager to settle this Santa Claus question once and for all.

Deeply immersed in the holiday spirit, Mom and Dad sang along with the car radio as Christmas music traveled along the snow packed roads, following us all the way home. "This one's for you, Kareen." Dad announced, catching my eye in the rearview mirror as he joined in song with the crooner.

"All I want for Chrithh muth is my two front teeth,
My two front teeth, my two front teeth.
All I want for Chrithh muth is my two front teeth
So I can withh you Merry Chrithh, muth."

Loaded down with packages and a box of groceries we paused behind Dad as he flicked on the light switch inside the front room door.

212

And there, illuminated before my very eyes was the truth I'd been seeking! Roger didn't know anything! There really, truly was a real Santa Claus!

All of us had been together in town that afternoon so how did these two shiny, blood red, chrome trimmed pedal cars get in the middle of our front room? And who, but the real Santa, would know just when we would leave and when we would return?

There could be only one explanation. The real Santa had delivered these magical gifts to my brothers.

Relief flooded over me, washing away all my cynicism. It must have also washed away some of my Christmas greed, because for the life of me, I can't remember what Santa left for me.

Chapter 16 - And the Next Day it Rained

The New Year began with a picnic at the Sand Hills. The outing had been our neighbor's idea. He thought we should take the occasion to enjoy the fine, unseasonably, warm weather that had descended onto the Montana plains that winter.

Mr. Meeks and Mother knew of the Sand Hills since they had grown up together in Pleasant Valley, but it was a new and exciting place for the rest of us. Linda and her brothers, Billy and Allen, were now classmates of ours and together we represented the third generation of homestead families to marvel at the mysterious qualities of this strange place so different from the prairie surrounding it.

Wandering in and out and through the sand formations was like exploring on the warm side of the moon. While our mothers spread the picnic lunch, we played without coats, as if it were May instead of the middle of a Montana winter. Dad and Bill lounged against the side of a small sand hill, soaking up the sun rays that bounced off surrounding sand pillars.

Simple family outings that did not require an admission charge, served as a welcome diversion from our routine on the ranch. Sometimes it was a car trip to Havre, Choteau or Black Eagle. Any town within a hundred miles that harbored former North Dakotans served as Dad's favorite Sunday destination.

The traveling to and fro could not have been much fun for Dad since the backseat continued to be an arena for sibling battles. Mother added to the stress by constantly demanding that he roll down his window or put out his cigarette.

"We can't breathe in here," she'd complain as the smoke and miles drifted by.

But Dad came alive when we finally arrived at the door of friends from days gone by. Storytelling and exaggeration went hand in hand as he and his buddies exchanged tales of their days as young men trying to make their way during the Great Depression.

Dad's stories made the depression seem to us, his offspring, less grim than it must have been for those who endured it firsthand. Not being able to find a job did not seem so bad when you compared it to traveling across country in an open boxcar. And being cold, with nowhere to sleep, was not so serious if a friendly policeman arrested you for loitering just so you could spend the night in a warm unlocked cell. And if you knew your charm and good looks could coax a kindhearted waitress to slip you a sandwich once in a while, then you didn't really have to worry about always having enough money to eat on.

Depression and laughter are words that don't seem to fit when used in the same sentence but, probably because they were young and free of all adult constraints, Dad and his friends remembered the time with fondness and good humor. It was only occasionally that they grew serious and recounted tales of women and children, cold and hungry in the back of a boxcar trying to get to some far off place where a job or a husband might be waiting. Or they might recount the tale of a rich middle age banker who had lost everything; money, position and family. And sometimes, with the false bravado that comes years later when the terror had lost its hold on their memories, Dad would tell of the mean and angry men that preyed on the helpless, the weak and the young.

But mostly it was about the good times. We kids would be drawn to the adult stories by the laughter. And no one enjoyed Dad's stories more than he, as his long, lanky frame gyrated with every punch line. Everyone in the house would be smiling and on the edge of their seat as Dad drew one story after another to a dramatic conclusion. Everyone, that is, except Mother, who freely admitted to having a stunted sense of humor.

"Bill, there are children listening," she'd remind him if the story was growing a little too graphic. Or, "I've heard that story a hundred times before and it changes every time he tells it."

Mom's disapproval only served to trigger Dad's laughter and 'one more' story. He was on a roll and the adventures tumbled out like marbles from an open leather pouch. With Dad's "Remember when…," we were off on another wild tale of 'Bulls' or 'Rubes' in the train yards and towns, or cooking in a hobo jungle somewhere along the Montana High Line.

Totally spent, Dad would head the car homeward in the dark of night a contented and happy man. Until Mother insisted that he roll his window down.

Mother was good at insisting; like the time she convinced Dad to take us swimming in the Marias River one warm summer evening. It had been one of those blistering days when, what little wind there was, dried your lips and eyeballs. The sun, hanging low in the western sky, was still radiating like a coil heater in January.

Dad protested. "I've worked all day and I'm tired." When that didn't register with his wife, he suggested that it was too far to go.

"Oh, it's only seven miles. Come on. The kids will love it and can't you just imagine how wonderful that cool water is going to feel?"

Finally Dad gave in and we piled into the car not knowing what to expect. The ride to the Marias was an exciting one. After about three miles the prairie began to break into gullies and coulees. We encouraged Dad to hit a few speed bumps which sent us squealing and flying off the sweaty backseat. He grew more cautious though as we approached Collins Hill.

It was a long, treacherous trail down to the river bottom that had to be negotiated with care. If a car picked up too much speed it was in danger of flying off one of the hairpin curves that wound around and down the side of the hill.

We learned something new about our Dad that evening. Maybe Mother already knew, but it was a big surprise for us to learn that our big, strong father was afraid of something.

We discovered that Dad was afraid of water and could not swim. Consequently, he was fearful for his kids as we splashed and dog paddled in the cool backwaters of the river.

"Jean, if those kids get out there too far I can't do one damn thing about it," he warned Mom as he stood near the bank, water sloshing around his boney ankles.

"Don't worry," she called back, "We'll be careful."

After we climbed back in the car, refreshed and cool, Dad relaxed. Heading back up the hill we interrogated him about his lack of swimming skills.

"How come you don't know how to swim, Dad?"

"Well, you know; there's not a lot of water in North Dakota," he answered as he ground the gears and pressed on the accelerator. "I just never had a chance to learn I guess."

"You could learn now," I insisted.

"Not on your life!" he told me with a firm glance in Mother's direction and that ended our first and last swimming trip to the Marias.

Trips beyond Montana's borders were rare and usually confined to family visits in North Dakota or St. Paul. Once, Mom, Dad and the boys went to the Oregon coast but I was in school at the time and was left behind, moving in with my teacher in the teacherage. And then there was the time we went back to Seattle to see Uncle Adolf who was in the hospital there.

We were still very small but I remember seeing tall buildings surrounded by a thousand shades of green and streets full of people that looked very different from our friends and neighbors back home. Innocently, Butch commented on the skin color of some of them which got my mother in trouble a few times.

"He's a little boy and doesn't know any better," one passerby told Mom. "But you should be teaching him better!"

One afternoon when Uncle Adolf was having a particularly bad day, Dad suggested that Mom take us to visit Mrs. Cook, our former landlady. I had never been on a bus before and, while eager for a new experience, I worried about finding our way back to Dad and the hospital.

We waited behind Mother's skirt; Butch clutching one of her hands and me the other as a huge vehicle rumbled down an incline and rolled to a stop right in front of us. The bus appeared to be bigger than Dad's grain truck but instead of climbing up into a cab, steps led upwards to a spacious platform filled with passengers. The best part was that we were surrounded by windows. With faces plastered to the glass, Mother gave us a running tour of the city. Hours later, after we were deposited back at the very spot we had left from I was convinced that every town should have at least one bus.

But as luck would have it, several years later, I was nearly killed by a bus.

We had just finished a reasonably good harvest, which provided a few extra dollars that Mom thought should be spent on a short family vacation to Glacier Park.

The first few nights we spent in the East Glacier Lodge, located at the eastern entrance to the park. At first my brothers and I were awed by the magnitude and elegance of the hotel. Surrounding the massive lobby, a forest of huge tree trunks held up a roof that soared miles above our heads. Warm, welcoming fires blazed in several large stone fireplaces.

But, as undisciplined farm kids are known to do, we were soon running wild, testing our courage as we edged out on to the balconies surrounding the lobby, racing through the halls and playing hide and seek among the overstuffed chairs and potted plants. Corralling us and keeping us under control meant that we were confined, along with our parents, to our sleeping room, which Mom and Dad could only stand so long.

What appeared to Denny, Butch and me to be a speedway was in reality a quiet connecting corridor for the main lodge and its west wing. It joined the two lodges at the second floor but was not quite level since the two buildings were not the same height. On each side of the long hall, were massive windows, each with its own writing desk where awestruck tourists, inspired by the snowcapped peaks and banks of wildflowers, could write a postcard home or add a page to their vacation journal.

At the time, the boys and I were unaware of the quiet ambiance of the place. We only knew that the sloped corridor was a great place to run and roll and race back up again. It must have been complaints to the management that put a stop to our fun because Dad soon appeared and escorted us back to our room.

The rest of our time at East Glacier Lodge was spent within arm's reach of our parents as we strolled together around the grounds. With her black and white camera, Mother snapped pictures of us in front of flower beds and totem poles. Whether or not it was planned or maybe suggested by the management, we soon moved on, traveling up to Many Glacier Hotel at the north end of the park.

This is where I had my encounter with a bus.

After a few days on the road with three kids, Dad realized that there was no such thing as a "restful" family vacation. It became clear to him that he needed to find energy burning activities for his youngest family members. So, while not inclined to hike for the fun of it, he signed us up for a trek to a glacier the following morning. Mom decided to stay behind with Denny, thinking that his small legs could not cover the couple of miles of rocks and ice that we would probably encounter.

As often is the case in the high mountains, it was a misty day, cold and windy, as we wound single file up and away from the hotel. The adults trudged along the trail, collars up and hats pulled down; but for kids on tour, the weather was perfect. Running, climbing and jumping, we had to be reined in continually by Dad or the tour guide. Both were probably convinced that at least one of us would end up being carried back down the mountain with a broken limb.

Eventually, and without incident, we arrived at the glittering glacier and the clear blue lake below it. I took some time, showing proper admiration for the masterpiece God had laid out before us and then decided to get a head start on our tour director. After all, I knew the way back to the hotel and could make it faster without his constant supervision.

Butch was not as quick as I and was forced to remain behind, his hand tightly gripped by our alert father. Somewhere behind me I heard Dad yell at me to slow down but I could tell him, if he brought the subject up, that I couldn't hear him because of the wind.

In half the time it took us to go up the trail, I crested the hill that lay just across the road from the hotel. Without thinking or looking, I bounded down the incline, heading for the main entrance.

I heard people shout and brakes scream as I went down onto the gravel and under the front of a red tour bus. Immediately I was surrounded by anxious faces and a weeping bus driver. Helping me to my feet, they leaned me up against the bus and examined my bumps and bruises. Luckily, the alert driver had managed to brake just in time, leaving me shaken but all in one piece. As the crowd disbursed, I pulled myself together, got my quivering limbs under control, shook the gravel out of my hair and made a snap decision.

As my Dad and brother came down the path towards me I decided that there are some things that your parents just don't need to know. An overly dramatic story about a little fall would explain the bruises and listening to a brief lecture by Dad, about "staying with the group" and it would all be behind me.

But Dad was not so easily fooled when it came to the picnics that Mother and Grandmother organized to celebrate some special occasion or just to do something different. He knew that picnics involved a lot of work.

"I have a picnic everyday out there on the tractor," he'd complain. "Can't we just relax once in awhile?"

Mom wasn't taking no for an answer. "I hardly think a baloney sandwich eaten on a tractor could pass as a picnic and besides, it'll be fun. The kids love picnics."

Sometimes we went to Gibson Park in Great Falls where us kids could feed the ducks, play on the playground equipment or get dramatic on the empty stage of the stately band shell that served as the central feature of the park.

Dad, my Uncle and Grandpa napped on blankets in the shade, oblivious to the comings and goings of their offspring. After cleaning up the picnic residue, Mom, Aunt Dawn and Grandma would discuss a variety of boring subjects such as; who liked Liberace and who did not. Mom and Grandma thought he was too prissy while Aunt Dawn was a dedicated fan. She sighted his candelabra, grand piano and tuxedo, as well as his amazing talent. Mostly we just rolled our eyes and ran off to a far corner of the park.

Our favorite picnic destination was Ryan Dam. Dad hated the place. Again, it was a water issue. The Montana Power company had created a lush, green picnic grounds on an island in the middle of the Missouri River. Dad planned on at least one of his children drowning every time we visited.

Farm families found the place a welcome respite from the wind and sun of the flat land. Just a few miles off the highway, a winding road led down into a deep canyon which was spanned by a massive dam. If the car windows were rolled down and the spillway open, you could hear the thunder of the falls as you dropped down into the wide crevice carved over many centuries by the cascading Missouri. Raging and roaring, the river split and poured around the island at the base of the dam.

Finding three parking spots for each of the family vehicles, everyone lined up behind open car trunks. We knew that there would be no playing or exploring until all the food and picnic paraphernalia had been packed down the stone steps and across the bridge to the island.

"If I catch you kids climbing down around that river, I'll skin you alive!" Dad threatened as he handed boxes off to Butch, Denny and me.

The Montana Power Company also had strict rules which were posted just overhead as you started across the bridge.

1. NO FIRES ALLOWED. (An all-electric kitchen, provided free of charge by the power company, stood in the middle of the island).

2. NO VISITORS AFTER 9 P.M. (The gates to the bridge were unlocked at ten in the morning and locked at nine in the evening).

3. DO NOT SWAY THE BRIDGE (A rule begging to be broken)

As visitors streamed across the bridge, there was always someone who felt obligated to see just how far the bridge would swing. Pressing forward and to the left with one leg then pressing in the opposite direction with the other leg caused the bridge to swing back and forth, over the raging river below. If you were big enough or had others to help you, the bridge would soon be swaying enough to illicit a few screams from the more cautious picnickers.

My brothers and cousins were too small to get much of a sway going but that didn't stop them from trying.

"Butch, stop that right now!" Mother would order as she packed a kettle of her famous chicken and noodles across the bridge. Too much swaying and she'd have chicken stock all over the bridge's narrow walkway.

Mother, always thinking ahead, had encouraged us to arrive early so we could get tables close to the cook house. Dad was thinking too. He knew that within a few hours, after one of his kids had been swallowed up by the Missouri River, he would have to pack all the boxes, empty kettles and dishes back across the bridge, up the stone steps to the waiting cars and finally back into the family kitchen. He grumbled continually, right up until naptime.

Depositing the last of our cargo on the closest picnic tables my brothers and I hit the rocks.

Dad's concerns were well warranted. Above the picnic grounds, up another set of stone steps, at the front of the island, were huge rock formations with a walkway for viewing the falls and the surrounding canyon walls. Below these ragged cliffs and boulders lay the rocks that locked the island in place and absorbed the never ending force of the river as it roared downstream. When Dad was awake and watching, we played on the rocks above. When Dad was napping or visiting we climbed over the barricades and explored the rocks below.

It's hard to overestimate the attraction that danger poses, especially when viewed through the eyes of young boys. Daring the river, without thought of death or drowning, we climbed around the driftwood and rocks with the spray of the falls in our faces.

For once, my parents were united in their concerns for our safety. To drive home their point, the grown-ups exchanged horror stories of foolish young people who had been swept away by the swift current, never to be seen again. Maybe their stories finally registered with me or maybe I just got older and wiser, but I began to realize that the river was a very real threat. Feeling a glimmer of responsibility for my brothers, I reverted to 'telling on them' whenever I thought they were growing too reckless. This pretty much alienated me from them for the rest of the day but at least we always got the boys off the island alive.

The State Fair in Great Falls, which usually fell around harvest time, was one of the few extravagances of the summer. While normally conservative with their resources, Mom and Dad came to the fair for a good time and planned on spending a little more freely than usual. Arriving about midmorning, we gathered around Dad and his wallet.

"Kareen, you take Jimmy. Here's ten dollars for the two of you. Butch and Denny, here's five for each of you and don't come back begging for more money."

"Why do I always have to take Jimmy?" I whined. "All he wants to do is go on the baby rides."

Mom wasn't buying my 'poor me' routine. "You'll have all afternoon to do what you want. But this morning, you're going to take him on some rides and that's final. I'll be in the flower barn if you need me."

"And I'll be playing Bingo in the Odd Fellow's booth. We'll meet in front of the grandstand at noon," Dad shouted after us as we headed for the midway.

We regrouped, as ordered, in front of the grandstand at noon. By this time, Grandma and Grandpa had arrived for the afternoon rodeo. Together, we trouped into the cook shack, found a table and proceeded to fill up on hamburgers and pie.

Because they had already spent all of their five dollars and because they knew that Grandpa was a soft touch, Butch and Denny sat on either side of him, complaining about how expensive all the good rides were.

Dad was not listening. "I don't want to hear it," he told them. As far as he was concerned, his wallet was closed.

My grandparents were sympathetic, agreeing that five dollars didn't go very far these days which, eventually, over my parents protests, resulted in three more five dollar bills being passed around, one for each of us, except Jimmy who would be attending the rodeo with the grown-ups.

Since I had spent my morning watching Jimmy go round and round in the baby cars or riding double with him on the merry-go-round, I still had most of Dad's five dollars left and was now feeling quite prosperous.

After lunch, we separated from the adults, with instructions to come to the grandstand when we got tired or ran out of money. Hitting the midway with my brothers, I was horrified to watch them blow most of their five dollars trying to win a toy gun by throwing wooden rings over milk bottles.

"Come on, you dummies," I demanded. "You can't win at those games. Dad says they're rigged."

"You don't know anything! We've seen lots of people win stuff," they argued as they continued to plop quarters down on the counter.

Finally, with only a few quarters left they decided to give up on the milk jugs and use the remainder of their money on the bumper cars.

I tagged along not knowing what to do with myself and my bulging pockets.

Behind the wheel, my brothers oozed self confidence as they gleefully smashed and bumped into my slow moving vehicle from every angle possible. Bang, from the left as Butch hit me in the side. Smack, from behind as Denny drove full force into the back of my stalled car. Frantically turning the wheel and pressing on my accelerator I tried to escape to a corner just as Butch circled back around and smashed into me head on. By the time we left the raceway they were feeling very cocky indeed.

But they were out of money again.

"How about loaning us some of yours," they begged. And just that quick, I was back in charge.

As we got older and our life experiences expanded, it became much harder to maintain the mystic of 'older sister'. I knew I was supposed to be smarter and more resourceful and braver than my little brothers but as we ventured beyond our ranch home, out into the big wide world, I felt less reliable as their life guide. New situations made it harder for me to convey an air of authority and poise. Of course I could fake it if I had to but, quite often, I was shown up for the weak-kneed, scared, little kid I really was.

Flying was one such occasion.

Looking back on it, I can't remember why Dad and Mother decided my brothers and I should have a plane ride. Money was always in short supply so why would they pay thirty dollars to hire a pilot to fly Butch, Denny and me out into the big skies of Montana? And I don't think either of them had ever been in a plane before, so why us and not them?

Maybe the barnstormers that occasionally came in low, buzzing our outbuildings and driving our chickens into a state of nervous molting, got us excited about flying. Maybe Butch or Denny had a burning interest in aviation that I was unaware of. Maybe I had carelessly suggested the possibility of a plane ride. But I don't think so.

Nevertheless, one hot, summer Sunday afternoon, we left Grandmother's yard early and headed out of town to the east. I assumed that we were taking the long way home; out the Green Roof road, but instead, Dad pulled into the local airport at the top of the hill.

Mom's eyes danced as she told us we were in for a wonderful adventure. "Your Dad and I think it's time you had an airplane ride," she announced enthusiastically as Dad exited the car and entered a small, cinderblock building.

For a fraction of a second we were in a state of shocked disbelief which just as quickly morphed into wild excitement, at least for my brothers. I will admit to being caught up in the moment but somewhere, deep in my subconscious, trepidation and dread were beginning to germinate.

Bravely, I smiled at the friendly pilot as he directed the boys to the backseat and helped me into the front, next to him. I was grateful that he acknowledged my rights, as the oldest, to the best seat and let myself believe that this would be a pleasant experience for all of us. How wrong I was!

"Take them out over the valley," Dad yelled, backing away from the plane. "They'll want to see the ranch buildings and the school if you can point them out."

"Will do!" the pilot shouted. The plane's propeller began to whirl and the motor roared as he helped us snap on our seat belts.

"Have fun!" Mother yelled from across the air strip. Both she and Jimmy waved exuberantly and with a confidence that I was not sharing.

The plane began to vibrate as it turned and lined itself up with the runway. "Now is the time to tell him I've changed my mind," I remember thinking. But it was too late. The wheels were leaving the ground and we were airborne.

Immediately transfixed, I watched the world change before my eyes. Dad, Mother, our car and the buildings below became small and insignificant as the horizon expanded and the world of sky and earth grew vast and borderless.

We swooped out over the hill, circling around Fort Benton. "I wonder if Grandma and Grandpa know we're up here," I thought as we banked over the town and headed directly north. Within minutes we were beyond the Teton and the river breaks. In a few minutes more the pilot was pointing out our ranch house below.

We came in low, right over the yard. Clark, our hired man, was on the back porch waving up at us. Butch and Denny were thrilled, shouting their enthusiasm from the back seat.

"Do it again! Do it again!" they hollered over the scream of the climbing engine.

We circled to the north, over the reservoir and came back, right over the shop, heading in a half roll for the school.

"Wow!" yelled the boys with every swoop and dive of the aircraft.

All the while I was turning green, inside and out.

Driven by my brother's wild enthusiasm, our pilot banked the plane over the school, tipped one wing toward the ground, circled back around, and then pulled the machine skyward just as we approached the building's roofline.

"I'm going to throw up," I announced quietly to no one in particular.

The pilot's reflexes had been quick and sure but for a moment, he looked perplexed and uncertain.

"What did you say?" he shouted over the roar of the engine.

"I said, I'm going to throw up."

Immediately he regained his composure and took charge of the situation.

"Not in my plane you're not!" he yelled as he reached across me and opened the door on my side of the aircraft. "Stick your head out!" he ordered.

I stared at him in stunned disbelief. "No, I can't!"

"You will or else! Stick your head out! Now!"

I resisted. The boys, forgetting about their excitement, were now focused on the drama playing out in the front seat. I was focused on the pilot's 'or else' and the squishy feeling rumbling around in my stomach.

"Do what he says!" the boys yelled from behind me.

As the vomit began to work its way up, I continued to fight eviction.

With one hand on the controls the pilot reached over, grabbed me by the shoulder and forced my top half out over the fields of Pleasant Valley.

"Oh, gross," the boys groaned as the wind sucked the contents of my stomach out into thin air, over the struts and past the back window.

Terrified, I tried to fight my way back into the plane.

"Not till you're finished!" the airman shouted, still forcing me to hang out over the prairie.

"I'm done, I'm done!" I shouted back. Stomach cleared, I was now getting angry. "He's going to kill me," I told myself. "What if my seat belt breaks loose?"

I had visions of punching him into oblivion if I could just get back into the plane but then I reconsidered. We needed him to get us back on the ground in one piece.

Finally, he pulled me back into the safe confines of the plane and handed me his handkerchief. "Feeling better?" he inquired sweetly.

"Yes," I snapped, wiping the remaining vomit from my face and giving him a glare that I hoped would wipe the big grin off his face.

"Well, you'll have a good story to tell your folks won't you?" His tone was kind and his smile infectious. "We better head for town before we have any more excitement up here."

The boys groaned and pleaded for more but our trip back was assured as we headed in a bee line for the airport. There were no more circles, swoops and rolls. But there was the landing yet to deal with.

Nervously I surveyed the tiny landing strip below us.

The pilot offered his assurance. "It'll be O.K.," he promised.

Even the boys grew quiet as plane and ground came together in one mighty burst of wind, wings and wheels, bringing us safely back to earth.

"How did it go?" Dad asked as he ran up to help lift us out of the cockpit.

"She threw up!" Butch said in disgust.

With a wink and a smile in my direction the understanding young airman came to my defense. "She did just fine!" he assured Dad. I smiled back, grateful for his efforts to restore my dignity.

All the way home the boys enthusiastically recounted every detail of their flight over Pleasant Valley. I, on the other hand, was quiet and thoughtful, wondering if I could somehow pinpoint the exact spot where my stomach remains might have landed.

And the next day, it rained.

Chapter 17 — To Be a Girl

I didn't know a thing about being a girl. I knew how to be a big sister; which, in a nutshell, was all about intimidation and bossing. And I was absorbing, without knowing it, how to be a mother, but the art of dolls and dresses never interested me. I had a doll of course, maybe several, but once I tired of tipping them back and forth to watch their eyes open and shut, I pretty much lost interest.

Mother did her best to add some femininity to my tomboy existence. There were the curls that she required me to sit still for as she wound my blond hair around her fingers in three inch ringlets, 'Shirley Temple' style. I hated those curls and told her so, many times.

When Mother tried to teach me how to embroider I just sat there in the middle of the kitchen and bawled. Tears coursed down my cheeks and dripped, in a random fashion, across the breadth of the hooped dishtowel. Sometimes I pricked my finger on purpose just to prove how inept I really was with a needle and thread.

Now blood mixed with the tears on the white cotton cloth in my hands. "I can't do this," I whined.

Patient, at first, Mother reassured me. "Of course you can. Just take your time."

It wasn't that I couldn't…I didn't want to. I wanted to go outside. I begged and pouted. Eventually Mom gave in and my morning sewing sessions were put on hold.

She dressed me up for trips to town in fluffy little dresses and black-paten shoes. It seemed to me, as I watched my cousin Vicky, several years younger than myself, being dressed by my Aunt in the same sort of frothy costumes, that there was some sort of competition going on about who had the sweetest little female in the family. Mother was doomed to lose.

I think I might have done better at girl stuff if I had had a big sister. My cousin Rachel, in Great Falls, a year or so older than me, was pretty and lady-like and could have shown me a thing or two. And there were my older, sophisticated cousins in St. Paul, but in both cases these young ladies were too far away to be of much help and it didn't seem to me that their city ways worked very well out on the ranch anyway.

And so, I was left to my own devices. I was happiest with the boys and doing boy things. There were the snake hunts at Uncle Alan's place, the unreliable raft that Bobby, Butch, Denny and I floated on the Garber reservoir and fights, always with boys, on the playground at school. Most of these fights were not the knock down drag out type where punches are thrown and eyes blackened. All the boys, except Roger, were younger and smaller than me so it was mostly about huffing and bluffing and maintaining order.

As I grew older, it wasn't that I left boyish pursuits; it was that the boys left me. More and more they went off with our male cousins and the neighbor boys, leaving me to entertain myself.

Books replaced male companionship. On days when the boys managed to escape without me I ventured into the world of words and pictures. On long hot summer afternoons I dropped down between our twin beds and lost myself in whatever reading material was on hand at the time.

In this exciting new world, I didn't need the boys or my parents. I could read whenever I wanted and about anything I might be interested in at the time. I used my own dimes for comic books and had my own library card.

Even after the lights were shut off at night I found a way to read. Sneaking Dad's flashlight out of the junk drawer in the kitchen, I created an illuminated reading grotto underneath my flannel blankets.

"You're going to ruin your eyes, young lady," Dad would warn. "And you'll be a grouch in the morning. Now give me that flashlight and go to sleep."

To learn more about girls, I tried to read about girls. But in spite of being my favorite series, what did I have in common with CheeWee, an Indian girl who lived in desert cliff dwellings? It was impossible to identify with Nancy Drew who always wore a skirt and had several girlfriends trailing after her from one mystery to the next. And what could I learn from Laura Ingles Wilder? She had only sisters to deal with. It was even hard to find girls in my book of Bible stories unless you counted the one that fished baby Moses out of the Nile River.

So, I resorted to gender neutral reading material. Grandma gave me books about the ponies of Chinquatique Island and Brighty, a mule that carried people to the bottom of the Grand Canyon. My favorite book was one Mom and Dad gave me for Christmas. It was all about words and their meanings with pictures to match. And, of course, there were my comic books, which I read from cover to cover and then stacked in piles around our shared sleeping quarters.

Perhaps worrying that her daughter would spend her whole life with her nose in a book Mother endeavored to expose me to different social situations. The first big event was my sixth birthday party.

Turning six in our family was sort of like turning twenty-one or something. It was a very big deal. There was the new bike from my grandparents and a super party held in the city park.

Being an ex-teacher and life-long resident of Chouteau County, Mother knew a lot of people who had kids our age and she must have invited every one of them to my party. For me it was like winning an Oscar, being elected President of the United States and winning the lottery all in one afternoon. There were too many kids, too many presents and probably too much sugar.

Eventually I fell apart. "I don't know any of these kids," I whined. "And that big boy over there is mean." I was overwrought.

"Stop being such a baby," Mother admonished. "He's Mrs. Vielleux's grandson. Just be nice to him and he'll be nice to you."

Mom wasn't listening. She probably thought I was just tired. But I really wanted to go home or, even better, I wanted everyone else to go home.

I did a little better at the wedding shower Mother hosted for my soon-to-be second grade teacher, Miss Dahl. Even though I had yet to meet the woman, Mom dictated that I should co-host. Dressing up, of course, was mandatory, along with keeping my voice down and smiling continually. Miss Dahl was gracious and outgoing but I knew that her praise for the gift I gave her was way over the top.

Days before the shower Mother sat me down with a discarded bottle, creamy beige paint and a paintbrush. The objective, as she explained it, was to cover the bottle with the paint. After the paint dried she had me cut and paste colorful decals around the bottle in a random fashion. I sensed that it was not the work of art she had hoped for but, once we stuck the sprinkler cork in the top of the bottle, it at least took on the appearance of something that might prove useful to a new bride.

"I think Miss Dahl really liked your present," Mom said as we sat together on the shady side of the house, enjoying the stillness of a late August afternoon. The shower guests were gone and it was not yet time to start supper. "I bet she'll make a wonderful teacher," she continued.

Mom's prediction turned out to be true but at the time, I only remember thinking how great it felt to be back in my jeans, there with Mom, alone on the cool stone steps with nothing, at least for the moment, to do. A soft breeze teased our hair as I leaned back into her ample chest. The pressure of being a "lady" evaporated like water on a hot sidewalk. Somehow I knew, that in spite of my awkward performance that afternoon, just being Mom's daughter was enough for her and that made life for me, very good indeed.

Living on a Montana wheat ranch provided limited opportunities to socialize with girls my own age. Since there were only three other girls in the whole valley, and since two of them had moved away, it was pretty much, to my way of thinking, a male world.

One bright spot was when Elmer and Irene's niece, Marsha, came for a week's visit each summer. Only a mile away, it was easy to get us together, either at our place or theirs, several times during that short stay.

Marsha was a town girl from eastern Montana and much more sophisticated than me or my rural friends. When I think of poise, I think of Marsha, but she was not above climbing with me, in and out of the pigpens or setting up a playhouse in an empty granary.

Staying overnight with Linda or the Garber girls also helped widen my social circle and exposed me to family cultures different, but not much, from my own.

For several summers after they moved away, Kay and Alice returned from wherever it was they had moved to, in order for their father to farm their place. Anxious to renew our kindergarten friendship, Kay and I pressured our mothers to get us together.

Since Mrs. Garber had to pass our place on her way to and from town, she sometimes picked me up for an overnight stay.

The Garber place was at the northeast end of Pleasant Valley, off the main road, far from neighbors, school and a long way from town. The house was not equipped with any of the conveniences that Grandpa was busily introducing at our place. Electricity had not yet reached them and water was carried from the cistern to the house in a bucket. Truth be told, the place was nearing the end of its usefulness as a family dwelling.

Come bed time, Kay, Alice and Bobby climbed up under the rafters and crawled into their individual sleeping spaces. I don't know how it worked when I wasn't there, but when I was, the girls got the spot by the tiny window at the south end of the attic. Crunched into the stifling heat of the loft, we crowded next to the open window, sucking up what cool night air might drift our way.

Dreamily, after Bobby and Alice fell asleep, Kay and I gazed out on a trail of stars that wound across an endless sky. Around the dilapidated little house, the land lay silent, empty and still, waiting only for the kiss of the morning sun to bring it back to life.

By all standards, it was a lonesome, forsaken spot. Instead of sitting out on the open prairie like our place, the ram shackled house and outbuildings were nestled into a shallow coulee, which affected my sense of space and distance. I had the comforting feeling of being cradled by the earth rather than being blown off it.

Montana's original inhabitants must have felt much the same way, as the place was littered with teepee rings. On the rim of one small hill up from the house, Alice, Kay and I inspected the stone circles. While Mr. Garber permitted hunting for arrowheads he warned us against disturbing the rings.

"They belong to the ages, kids," he'd tell us.

He needn't have worried. Encased by centuries of blowing dirt and overgrown with bunch grass, the stones were locked in place, their presence a reminder that others had come before us and thought of this wide space under the sun as home, just like we did.

Threading our way up through the coulees we waded into an ocean of waving grass. Charting a course up and over small hills, with the wind always at our backs, we lost ourselves in the vastness of the prairie, mere specks in a golden sea, broken only occasionally, by what we believed to be long ago abandoned buffalo wallows.

These wallows sort of resembled sand traps on a golf course but instead of sand, they were filled with a powdery dust worked free of the surrounding grasses by the rolling and thrashing of thousands of buffalo over thousands of years.

In every way, Linda's home was the exact opposite of Garber's. The Meeks' place, smack dab in the middle of the valley, was on the main road to town. The house was solidly built, large and comfortable. Rich wood wainscoting surrounded a formal dining room. The focal point of the front room was an elegant fireplace and a picture window that opened onto the front porch. At the back of the house was a long enclosed porch which ran the entire length of the house with stairs leading down to a full basement. Upstairs, on the second floor, were two bedrooms; one for Linda and one for her brothers, as well as the doorway to an attic. In spite of all these amenities, the Meeks family, just like the rest of the neighborhood, had to go out the back door to relieve themselves.

One could classify Linda as my 'best friend' but since neither of us had anyone else to choose from, this was a pretty hollow designation. Our lives were very similar. We had been born less than a month apart. Her Dad and my Mother had gone to school together. Both Linda and I were the oldest with younger brothers and both of our Dads were named 'Bill'.

And both of us proudly wore the label of 'Tomboy' and dressed the part; as long as our parents didn't interfere. It was only natural then for me to assume that even though Linda was smarter than I was and had a room of her own, there was probably very little she could teach me about being a girl.

Horses were nearly a profession at the Meeks' place. All of them had their own horse and everyone rode. They rode in parades and rodeos. They rode to school and just for fun. While a stay at the Garber's was mostly about exploring on foot, a visit to the Meeks' place was spent, primarily, on a horse.

One of my best days with Linda was a ride westward from their place to the back door of the Teton River. With her Mom's lunch bulging in our saddle bags, we headed out across the grain fields, the late morning sun rising behind us. By noon we had reached a rocky rim above a nearly dry riverbed.

"We can have our lunch down there by that old cottonwood," Linda indicated, turning her mount's head toward the steep bank.

The shade looked inviting but I wasn't so sure about getting down the hill. I'd seen it done a dozen times before in cowboy movies; horses charging down the side of a cliff, rocks rolling and cowboys whooping, but since I always rode on flatland or, at the most, gradually sloping hills, I was not so sure I could handle the maneuver. And I didn't know the horse.

Grandma had always impressed upon me the importance of understanding what your horse was thinking and what it was capable of.

"Are you sure this horse can get down there?" I asked Linda.

"Sure, just give him his head and he'll bring you right on down," she shouted over her shoulder as she disappeared over the bank.

Cautiously I rode up to the rim, watching as shale broke loose and rolled out from under her horse's sliding hooves.

Finally, suspecting that it was not the horse that I was worried about, Linda grew impatient. "Come on, it's easy," she yelled from below.

I was still unsure. "How about coming out? Are you sure we can get back up out of there?"

"Ya, of course, or I wouldn't have come down. Come on. Just do it."

Linda could act so superior sometimes.

"Well, this is what happens when I'm not in charge," I thought to myself. Now there was nothing left to do but turn my mount's head downward and hold on.

With a kick to its withers, a snap of the reins and a weak "giddy up", we headed downhill at a thirty degree angle. Forcing myself to do what I knew had to be done I leaned back in the saddle as far as I could, creating, as nearly as possible, a level plane of horse and rider. And even though I knew it was very 'un-cowboy' like and that Grandma would not approve, I hung on to the saddle horn as if my life depended on it.

"Keep your balance," I heard Grandma whisper from somewhere deep in my memory bank.

Time slowed down and the world shrank to just this steep riverbank and the horse beneath me. Rocks cracked and broke loose out from under us as my horse half galloped and half slid, back haunches collapsed underneath him, downward, head first to the river bottom below.

As my mount cantered forward, across the grassy bottom, a sense of bravado replaced my fears. In an instant it became clear to me why cowboys did so much whooping as I let fly a few whoops of my own. But then, turning my pony back towards the cliff, ready to gloat over what we had just accomplished, I learned a powerful truth.

I learned that our minds can play tricks on us, magnifying problems and obstacles until we are nearly paralyzed with fear and uncertainty. Looking back at the drop-off, I realized that the cliff was not so high and the bank was not all that steep, that my riding skills had been adequate and that I could trust my mount. Still harboring some small trepidation about riding back up out of the river bed, I considered this new revelation and immediately knew that if my horse could get me down the cliff, he could definitely get me back up.

It was time to relax. Linda had already dismounted and planted herself in the shade of the half dead cottonwood. Relieved that I had, at the very least, managed to match Linda's horsemanship skills, I ambled over, confident and cocky.

"Wow. That was fun!" I exclaimed. Linda just smiled and handed me one of Eleanor's sandwiches. Together by the riverbank I realized that it didn't matter if we were girls, tomboys, smart or not so smart; we were best friends.

I understood that girls turned into women and so I watched the hired girls, the neighbor ladies and my aunts. Some of what I saw, I did not approve of. Sometimes these girls, once grown, were too bossy. Some were too critical or worried too much. But from each of them, especially my aunts, I learned something about being female.

Occasionally, if Mom and Dad had to be gone overnight, they'd take us to stay with Uncle Allen and Aunt Bea. Their place was even more remote than the Garber place and just as primitive when it came to household conveniences. It must have been a hard place for a city woman like Aunt Bea, with the closest neighbors five or more miles away, the never ending work of chopping wood, carrying water and caring for her two boys, and now, new baby Billy.

Though Dad had high hopes that this rented farm would give his older brother and his new family a fresh start, it seemed that Uncle Alan was not taking much of an interest. Hauling grain to town often turned into an excuse to stop at the Palace for a beer.

Aunt Bea was a smoker and a coffee drinker. After the wicks of the oil lamps were trimmed and lit and all seven of us tucked into bed, she poured herself a cup of lukewarm coffee from the pot on the back of the wood stove; planted herself at the kitchen table and lit up a Camel.

Later, padding out to the kitchen in my pajamas, she invited me to sit with her as she waited for Uncle Allen to come home. I guess she was lonely and probably enjoyed having another female, regardless of how young, to visit with.

I asked her questions about city life, about Roger and Ronnie's Dad back in St. Paul and about meeting Uncle Allen. She told me about parties and dancing and divorce.

Sometimes I stayed there with her, girl talking, late into the night as we stared out into the darkness watching for that lone set of headlights we knew would be Uncle Allen driving himself home, drunk and broke, once again.

Staying, even for short periods of time, in the homes of other families, did teach me a few things about being a girl. I noticed that some husbands and fathers treated me better than they treated their own women. I noticed that some girls worked awfully hard, without much success, at trying to please their Dads.

It occurred to me that being a girl sometimes meant waiting for a man who didn't always come home. I noticed that some men were short-tempered and unreasonable with the females under their roof.

Over the years, I came to understand that not all men are the same. While I knew that my Dad ruled the roost, he did it with love, acceptance and forgiveness. Exposure to other families and circumstances taught me that some men ruled by intimidation and fear. And some didn't rule at all.

Eventually, I realized that girls learn a lot about being girls, good and not so good, from the most important man in their young lives; their Dads.

Chapter 18 — *Family Values, Pass it on*

As with most kids who grow up on a ranch, work, games and fun often overlap. This toxic combination proved to be a painless way to instill a work ethic in unsuspecting farm youngsters.

Decorating the outhouse walls was a creative activity as well as a chore assigned to the kids in our family as soon as they could hold a pair of scissors in their hands.

With stacks of old magazines gathered from Grandmother's house and our own back porch, we searched the pages, looking for pictures we judged to be of interest to those who were regular users of our outdoor toilet facility.

The little cubicle stood out from the other rundown farm buildings since it got a new coat of white paint, inside and out, every year. Grandpa was usually the one who called our attention to the condition of the pictures tacked up on the inside walls of the structure. He maintained that the illustrations should be changed regularly. I guess he liked the place to be entertaining as well as clean.

"Put up something about the election," Dad might advise.

"Put up some flower pictures," Mom suggested as she helped us prop open the outhouse door with a rock.

With our stack of neatly trimmed magazine photos from *Life*, *Look*, and *The Saturday Evening Post*, the boys and I squeezed inside. We knew we had to work fast since the outhouse was always in demand. First, we recklessly pulled the old pictures down from the walls and deposited them in the nearby garbage barrel.

Since I was the tallest, it was my job to climb up on the 'one seater' in order to tack pictures up as close to the roof line as possible. Butch and Denny made sure that the lower half of the north and east walls were covered, like wallpaper, with current event photos, tractor advertisements, and baseball pictures.

Together, the boys, Mother and I stood outside the open door admiring the completed project. "It sure looks nice doesn't it, Mom?"

"Yes it does," she replied heading for the kitchen. "I think your Grandfather will be pleased."

Springtime brought a very special package. This package could not be delivered by our mailman but had to be picked up in town. The call would come over the telephone and Dad would head for the post office returning with a large flat cardboard box with holes in the top. Cheeping and scrambling sounds came from within.

"Open it. Open it!" we'd shout as we crowded around the box.

Dad soon had the top off and there inside were the sweetest, fuzziest little yellow chicks any child could ever imagine. There were dozens of them, all squirming over and under and on top of each other.

"Oh, they're so cute," we'd croon in unison. "I want to hold one."

"Don't get too attached," Mom warned. "You'll be eating them this fall."

But we paid no mind. For the moment we enjoyed stroking their silky soft feathers and plump little bodies. Fall was a long way off.

Sometimes, if it was an especially cold spring, the little chicks would spend their first few days in the house, in front of our open oven door.

When Mother finally deemed it was time for them to go outside, we helped her move the chicks under the brooder, which was a tin tent, low off the floor of the chicken house. At the peak of the tent was a low wattage light bulb that radiated enough BTUs to keep the chicks toasty warm.

Comfortable and well-fed, the charming little chicks, within days, began to turn into chickens. The brooder roof had to be raised as the chickens grew taller. More feed was required and filling their water jug became a never-ending chore. I was beginning to lose interest.

I learned a lot about chickens in those early years. I learned that they roosted in the evening and got up before dawn. I learned that some were for eating and some were for laying. I learned that one rooster could keep a lot of hens happy. I learned to listen for a badger or a coyote in search of a chicken dinner. And I learned that there is nothing nastier than chickens unless it was cleaning out the chicken roost, a job that Mother had a hard time convincing anyone to help her with.

Pregnancy didn't slow Mom down much, at least that I could notice, but since Grandpa and Dad were intentionally unavailable, and she was in no shape to do it herself, the nasty job fell to my brothers and me.

The chicken roost was an ugly place, separate and apart from the chicken house. Poles were stair-stepped across the width of the shack which allowed the chickens to roost in formation, sort of like a church choir. Everything the chicken had eaten all day was deposited on the floor below and, over a period of time, began to pile up in disgusting white and gray mounds on the wood floor.

"It's gross!" I'd complain. "It makes me creepy crawly all over."

"Stop your whining and just get to it," Mom ordered handing me a short handled hoe. "Get back there in the corners and scrape it towards me and I'll rake it out the rest of the way."

It was a filthy job. Scraping up the dry manure raised all kinds of gray ugly dust and bumping one of the poles over-head resulted in poop in your hair.

As we scraped the chicken manure towards the door, Mother shoveled the stuff into buckets and then carried them to the garden where she scattered the contents helter-skelter around her growing vegetables. "Best fertilizer money can buy," she'd announce as we escaped to the water trough and washed ourselves head to toe.

Yes, I was learning to hate chickens. I hated gathering eggs. I hated washing dried chicken poop off the eggs. I even hated going in the chicken house and only did it under the sternest of threats.

But by late summer, it was time to rid the barnyard of the dirty, pesky birds and turn them into something I really liked; fried chicken.

Butchering chickens was a barbaric process, sort of like creating our own little horror movie. The chickens knew something was up as Mom moved into the pen, snatching one after another, like fish in a barrel. There was frantic squawking and clucking as she calmly maneuvered her long, sturdy hook around the chicken's leg, gave it a yank, pulling the surprised bird off the ground as she gathered both of their legs up in her other hand. Always insisting that wringing their necks was too cruel, Mom handed the doomed fryer off to one of us kids who had the difficult job of getting the victim to the chopping block.

The birds did not go quietly. Wings flapping and beak snapping at our exposed body parts, we carried the heavy, struggling bird, by its feet, head down, at arm's length over to our Dad who, with one good clean chop of the axe, ended the protest. Blood and flopping followed.

"That's just a reflex reaction," Dad assured us as the chickens, minus their heads, chased us around the yard. "They didn't feel a thing."

As the day wore on, it became an assembly line; snatch, carry, chop and flop. After a while, the killing became mechanical and automatic. With twenty or thirty dead chickens scattered around the yard, we moved into phase two.

Buckets of boiling water were carried out onto the back step. As we gathered up the dead birds, Mother dipped them into the steaming pots and passed them off to the rest of us for plucking. As the water cooled and the last chicken was plucked clean, Mom and Dad began the singeing. By now, a roaring fire was going in the garbage barrel with stacks of old newspapers and paper bags nearby.

This part of the process was too dangerous for kids but it was exciting to watch our parents work like fire eaters in a carnival. Grabbing a newspaper, giving it a stiff twist and then lighting it in the fire, they moved the flame up, around and over the dead bird, burning off any remaining feathers and then, dropping the burning paper back into the garbage barrel just before the flames raced up their shirt sleeves. One burning paper bag up the back side and between the drumsticks; another fire brand around the front over the breast and under the wings then, with a splash, the chicken was dropped into a galvanized tub of ice water.

Next, the tub was lugged into the middle of the kitchen floor. The table had been covered with freezer wrap and, one by one, Mother cut and wrapped piles of chicken parts for storage in our locker at the meat market in town. As a reward for our labor, she set a pot to boiling on the stove and dropped in a few chicken feet for an afternoon snack.

"Fried chicken tonight," she promised and without remorse or any misgivings, we'd devour, at the supper table, the victims of our morning labors.

The experience and emotions of death were an integral part of our childhood. In addition to butchering chickens, hogs, and cows there was the elimination of predators as well as grieving over lost or dying pets. The baby owls or rabbits Dad would bring home from the field after unintentionally plowing up a burrow or nest, oftentimes died within hours. Baby calves died in blizzards, horses died of old age and baby birds died if we were careless enough to disturb their nests in the shelterbelt.

While our parents and grandparents often enlisted our assistance in the ranch ritual of killing and death, they insisted we be excluded from the other end of life, the miracle of birth.

On a ranch, something was always being born but as far as I knew, baby animals just sort of popped up out of the ground, like cornstalks or pumpkins. In the opinion of our parents and grandparents, exposing kids to the birth of a colt or a calf might generate questions about how the baby got into its mommy's stomach in the first place. And there was the added concern that our young minds might be warped if we witnessed the struggle and trauma of birth. So, by joint decree, the birthing process was off limits for us kids.

Working beside my parents we learned to pitch in and do our share. That was as close as we came to activities with our Dad. As much as he loved baseball I don't ever recall him playing catch with one of my brothers. As much as he enjoyed reading, I don't ever remember him reading me a story. According to Dad there wasn't a lot of time for playing on a ranch. Kids were put to work when needed and were expected to entertain themselves the rest of the time.

But he did, unwittingly, draw us into his world of music and politics. These were Dad's passions and he counted on the radio to bring the sounds of both, right into the middle of our kitchen.

Life went on uninterrupted if music was coming in over the airwaves but when the news came on, we knew it was our job to be quiet or go play somewhere else. To Dad, news of Truman sacking McArthur, the latest election results, or the newest threat of Joseph Stalin was of primary importance. If one of us had lost an eye to a B.B. gun, or if Mother had a grease fire on the stove, we should not expect any help from him until the newscaster signed off for the night.

When we visited Great Falls during an election season we might find ourselves backed up behind Dad, along the curb of Central Avenue, listening to the persuasive campaign propaganda blasting from a bull horn wired to the top of a moving vehicle. To our dismay, he would oftentimes be drawn into political discussions with other men in the crowd who were just as interested in politics as he was.

The conversation remained civil, polite and short if both were of the same persuasion. If he ran into someone of opposite opinions, the discussions could get lengthy and loud. Mother's strategy, in such situations, was to drift off to finish her shopping, leaving us to deal with moving Dad along to the Johnson Hotel where we could read comic books while he continued to press his point of view.

When Election Day finally arrived my parents took turns voting at the schoolhouse. Dad usually went first then returned to watch us kids while Mom went to cast her vote. During her absence he, a first generation American, took time to reverently explain to his young family, the voting process and what a privilege it was to be able to live in a free country.

"They can't vote in Russia," he'd inform us. It occurred to me that Russia must be a very sad, unhappy place with children turning on their parents and prisoners freezing in Siberia.

Dad was a patriot to the core. "Just count your lucky stars that you live in the United States," was the

256

closing summation to every one of his Election Day lectures.

"Well, I cancelled you out," Mom teased upon returning from the voting booth.

Aware of the rumor that his mother and father-in-law were Democrats and knowing Mom prided herself on being an independent thinker, gave Dad reason to believe this might be true.

But voting, for our Dad, was a serious affair. "If you spent more time learning about the issues," he'd admonish, "you'd know how to vote."

As a former teacher, Mother was more concerned with how the English language was used than how you might vote. From a young age we were taught that our words should be carefully chosen. We could say "burp", but not belch, and stomach was to be used instead of belly. "Stinker," as in, "someone let a stinker," was allowed but not "fart". The other "F" word did not even exist as far as I knew, until the day I heard it used on my little brothers by a town bully.

Dad's language was also monitored carefully and corrections made as needed. Cussing by Dad or the hired men was not allowed anywhere near her children's ears. Sometimes, just for fun, while riding home on a cold winter's night, Dad might transition from a racy Norwegian ditty into the English version.

"Bill, there are children in the car," she'd remind him. He'd just laugh and sing another verse.

Music turned the world for my Dad. In his mind, there was nothing finer than dancing the "Tennessee Waltz" with his wife or a Polka with one of his sisters. He came to his marriage with a violin and added, over the years, a string harp, a mandolin and an organ. For

Christmas one year, Mom bought him an accordion. She considered this to be one of the greatest blunders of her adult life.

Dad usually got the urge to put a tune together sometime around the supper hour. At first we were drawn to the new instrument like gamblers to a race track. We expected that our Dad could find his way around the keys and buttons of the accordion just as smoothly as he played his old violin.

With a couple of snaps, the big, black case came open. Inside; rich, green velvet lining showcased a beautiful piece of musical engineering trimmed in Mother of Pearl inlay and intricate scrolling and flourishes around the bellows. Dad's fingers must have been itching and the musical side of his brain twitching, as he lifted it up out of its case and hung it over his wide shoulders. We waited in awed anticipation.

But nothing could have prepared us for the clamor and disharmony of a novice accordion player. As with all his instruments, Dad played by ear; working out each tune laboriously, note by note, a painful process for anyone within earshot of the musician. After experiencing the first few bars of *'Red River Valley'* played over about nine times, we melted away like honey on a hot biscuit.

But we could not escape that easily. It was cold and dark outside. If only the kitchen was further from the living room. We covered our ears. We grimaced. We made several quick trips to the outhouse. We shivered on the back porch. Mom encouraged us to be diplomatic and patient.

"Bill, supper's on the table," she would call sweetly.

"I've just about got it, Jean. Just give me a few more minutes."

The weeks rolled by. Our nerves turned to a tangled mass every evening about suppertime. Mother's patience was waning, both with our constant complaints and Dad's obsessive practice sessions.

"Bill, for God's sake, that's enough for one night," she'd call from the kitchen.

But Dad struggled on, trying to match the 'umpa pas' of the buttons with his finger work on the keys, all the while expanding and collapsing the bellows with enough vigor to keep both buttons and keys belting out a recognizable melody. It wasn't easy.

Mother could stand it no longer. With a half peeled potato in one hand and the paring knife in the other, she finally marched into the front room.

"Bill!" We just can't stand it! Put that thing away!"

Maybe there was something in the way that Mom wielded the knife that convinced Dad to put his accordion away for a few months or maybe it was time for spring work to begin. Whatever the reason, we were relieved and grateful.

When you think about it; Dad and Mom's generation was the first to have music at its fingertips. Grandma told us that in her day, tunes were passed from person to person. She and her sisters would pump new acquaintances or new hired men to teach them songs that had not yet arrived in the Idaho territory. Warm summer evenings were spent on the front porch of her childhood home learning and perfecting new melodies which they in turn would pass on to others.

In one of their good years, Grandpa bought Grandma a Victrola which sat in a corner of the parlor (the one with the chairs we could not sit on and the piano no one knew how to play). It was an elegant piece of furniture with a turntable inside and a turn crank on the outside. Though there were stacks of heavy black records stored in a side cabinet I never heard one of them played.

But with movies, car radios and '78' record albums, music became instantaneously available. Pop tunes were promoted and learned by a nation in unison. Dad knew the words to every song he ever heard and sang them as the occasion demanded.

He sang *'Good Night Irene'* to tease Mother about our neighbor lady, whose slim, attractive appearance occasionally stimulated bouts of green-eyed jealousy in our levelheaded Mother.

He sang *'Springtime in the Rockies'* as a love song to Mom when he was feeling amorous. He knew all the words to *'The Blue Skirt Waltz'* and he sang *'Put Another Nickel In, In the Nickelodeon'* to entertain his kids in the backseat of our rolling Chevrolet.

While music and politics were important to Dad, and Mother appreciated proper language skills and her flowers, we kids were avid fans of the Sears and Montgomery Ward catalogues which arrived twice each year, springtime and fall.

Fights ensued over whose turn it was to look at the bulky books that were filled with everything a person ever dreamed of owning. While I found the clothes at the front of the catalog interesting, I hurried through the underwear, household and hardware offerings and turned directly to the toy and book sections.

"I want one of those, and one of those and that," I'd point out to Mom as I planned ahead for my upcoming birthday.

"Are you sure you've picked out enough stuff?" she'd ask sarcastically.

Once, when I either had everything I wanted or I suddenly became less self-centered than usual, it occurred to me, as I browsed through the book section, that a new Bible would make a good gift for Mom's birthday. I went to my brothers with the idea and for their financial support. They had reservations.

"Bibles are hard to read," Butch protested.

"She doesn't have time to read," Denny reminded me.

Undeterred, I piled our stack of coins out on the oil cloth covering the kitchen table, right beside the order form. "Do we have enough?" I asked Dad as he helped me fill out the paperwork.

"Well, you're a few dollars short, but I haven't gotten Mom anything yet so I'll pitch in and it will be from all of us, O.K.?"

"Do you think she'll like it?" Always a tightwad, I wanted to be sure our money was spent wisely.

"I can't think of anything she'd like more," he reassured me. "She'll love it."

The arrival of the mailman became the central focus of our existence that second week of January. Finally, Mr. Archer handed us our long awaited package and the three of us raced to the shop.

"Dad, it's here! Let's give it to Mom right now!"

"Just let me get the grease off my hands first, "he responded.

Mom's eyes glowed with anticipation as she unraveled the black book from its brown paper wrappings.

"This is a wonderful gift," she exclaimed as she leafed through the gilt edged pages.

"And we paid a dollar extra to get your name printed on the front," Butch boasted.

"Do you like it?" Denny wanted to know.

"I love it! I've wanted a new Bible for ages," she whispered, with eyes moistening.

"It was Kareen's idea," Dad offered. "She picked it out all by herself."

Puffed up with so much pride that my blouse was near to bursting, I accepted her hugs and Dad's pat on the back. It was the first time I understood my Grandmother's axiom that it is always more fun to give gifts than receive them.

It was another such mail order that gave me pause and caused me to consider Dad's future role in raising his oldest daughter.

My first pair of pedal pushers had arrived the same way as Mother's Bible had; by mail, from Sears.

"Oh, they're a perfect fit," Mom exclaimed as she turned me around relishing the fact that she had finally gotten me into something besides jeans. "And you look so cute. Let's go show your Dad."

But Dad was not impressed. In fact, he seemed a little hostile.

"They better not get one inch shorter!" he fired off in Mother's direction as he circled the tractor, grease gun in hand.

Feeling spurned but not understanding why, tears began to flow as we turned back towards the house.

Wondering out loud, I asked Mom why Dad was mad at me.

"He's not mad at you, Honey. He just wants to be sure that you grow up to be a good girl," she assured me.

What growing up to be a 'good girl' and pink pedal pushers had in common I was not quite sure, but somehow, I was beginning to get the idea that Dad would be managing my life much differently than he did my brother's. Gradually, I was being molded to his standards of decency and morality without knowing why it was important or even how it would affect my growing up years.

While Dad took responsibility for guarding my virtue, Mother put herself in charge of fostering a sense of integrity in her children. I learned, the hard way, that lying and stealing would not be tolerated.

"How did this ball get in the back window?" Mom demanded as she cleaned out the car. Her tone of voice led me to believe that she already knew the answer to her question.

Quickly I calculated the consequences I was facing. I could lie, but I really didn't have a good story prepared. Or, I could tell the truth and if convincing enough, perhaps turn her apparent anger into, at a minimum, understanding.

As usual, I overestimated my verbal skills.

"That's stealing, Kareen, and, to top it off, disobedience. I told you plainly that you were not to take that ball home, didn't I? And you did it anyway!" Her accusations were basically, but not totally, on target.

263

I sputtered and tried to argue. She was being unfair. In my book, taking a ball that I found in a dump was not stealing. But you could never tell my Mom a thing. She was so darn unreasonable at times.

It all started with a pleasant afternoon drive to the Humphrey place. While Mom and Kay shared pie and coffee at the kitchen table and my brothers paired up with the Humphrey boys, I was left on my own. I decided to scout out their dump.

Every ranch had one; a coulee, some distance from the buildings that was used as a place to discard unwanted objects to be burned or buried or left to decay and rot away. Old bed frames, rusting car bodies, antiquated pumps, worn out tires, dilapidated household goods and broken toys piled up in layers, each representing a generation from homesteaders to the current occupants of the place.

And that's where I found the ball. I could tell by its scabby exterior that it had probably been in the dump for quite awhile but, in spite of that, it was in fair condition. Knowing full well that just taking the ball would be wrong and that Mother would not approve, I carried it up to the house and asked her if I could take it home.

"No, of course not," she informed me in no uncertain terms. "It belongs to someone else."

The word "no" did not often register with me and was definitely not valid unless challenged at least once or twice.

"But I found it in the dump!" I argued.

"I said no, and I mean no, now go play," she ordered turning away from my protests and back to Kay and her cherry pie.

"Oh, let her have it," I heard Kay whisper. "The boys will never miss it."

As the screen door banged shut behind me, I heard Mom reinforcing her directive. "No, she has to learn that she can't have everything she sees."

"I'll show her!" I told myself as I crept around to the far side of the car, opened the back door and hid the ball under my jacket in the rear window.

But I forgot to take it out of the car and now Mom had found it and there was a price to be paid. I cringed when I considered the possibilities. As usual, I could barely imagine the cruelties my Mother was able to dream up to ruin my life.

"We are going back to the Humphrey's right now and you will return this ball to Mrs. Humphrey, tell her you stole it and then apologize," she announced without a hint of pity in her voice.

"No, Mom. I can't. I'll die first."

"You can and you will, young lady. Now, get in the car."

There was nothing to do but capitulate. I believed my case was sound. I was willing to admit that I had disobeyed but I didn't steal the dumb ball, of that I was convinced. But Mother wasn't interested in truth or justice. All she wanted to do was humiliate me. I would not forgive her for as long as I lived I promised myself. I sat, silent and sulking all the way to the Humphrey place.

She marched me into Kay's kitchen; I said my piece as instructed and she marched me out again. With head hanging, totally mortified, I thought I sensed a hint of sympathy from Mrs. Humphrey as she accepted my apology but, in a case such as this, I knew that grown-ups always stick together.

Of course Dad had to hear all about my humiliation and even my grandparents had to be told. There was no escaping the cruel hand of Mother's law, until finally, at bedtime, she sat me down and talked me through the whole ugly episode. Crying together, we each conceded enough points that we found room for forgiveness and reconciliation on both our parts.

With each birthday, I realized that the moral issues were just going to keep coming. There was the movie that everyone was talking about, at least when they thought kids were not paying attention. Usually we all went to the movies together but for 'The Outlaw', Mom and Dad had Angie come down and stay with us.

When they returned home, I could tell Angie was anxious to hear all about the movie but Mom and Dad were pretty tight lipped, rolling their eyes in our direction.

This was a signal I understood well. It indicated that there was something they did not want their children to hear; things that would have to be discussed when we were not around.

Angie got the hint and so the most I got out of the discussion was that there was a lot of rolling around in the hay or some such thing. The word "sex", a word I still did not understand, was mentioned in a whisper.

This vocabulary deficiency was not my fault. I had seen that same word underneath a picture of a swimsuit clad model somewhere in a 'Life' magazine awhile back and inquired as to its meaning. Mother's definition had been pretty sketchy. As near as I could understand, it had something to do with attractive women.

And, to my mind, Jane Russell was definitely attractive, even in that torn blouse and with a straw hanging out of her mouth. But I could not, for the life of me, figure out what all the fuss was about. "For gosh sakes," I thought to myself. "It's just a girl in a haystack." I'd found myself in a few haystacks before and it was no big deal.

I had no idea where Mother and Dad were getting all these rules and opinions but I had observed that most grown-ups pretty much had the same outlook as my parents on what was and was not acceptable behavior in our valley community. There were a few exceptions of course; like our married neighbor, a few miles to the north, who got involved with wild women every once in awhile and the Chouteau County resident, far to the east of us, who shot his neighbor dead in a heated argument over well water. But on the whole, the rules and manners we lived by, seemed for the most part, to be universal.

But once Mom and Dad started reading the Bible every night, I got a new perspective on the formation of a moral code that, over time, evolved, rather than was simply dictated by the prevailing culture, current circumstances or by their peers.

I don't know what triggered their sudden interest in Bible reading. Maybe it was the friendly visits to our home by the new minister, Mr. Hanley and his wife, or maybe it was the fact that we were now attending Sunday School. Or, more likely, as I look back on it, maybe they were searching the Scriptures for answers to tensions and problems that were beginning to impact our family circle.

Whatever they were searching for, I wanted to understand it as well. So, if the house wasn't too cold and the boys were asleep, I left my bed, crept across the front room floor and quietly planted myself just outside their bedroom door.

The reading lamp, hanging from the headboard, cast a warm glow around my parents as they lay in bed, reading and discussing Bible verses. Mom did most of the reading and responding. Dad interjected with questions or his interpretation of what he thought a passage might mean. This did not seem to me to be a routine exercise, but a serious probing for truth and answers to life's big questions.

Crouched there, against the living room wall, quiet as God's own whisper, I shamelessly eavesdropped on my parent's private spiritual journey. Sometimes, I felt a pang of guilt, but the questions seemed so important and the language so compelling that I had to be there. I wanted to know what Mom and Dad were looking for. Was there some sort of magic or wisdom within the pages of that Book?

Was it courage they were seeking as they debated striking out on their own, leaving the ranch and my grandparents to fend for themselves?

How is faith involved when there are seven mouths to feed? Alone or together, as children of the depression and a world war, they were used to living on the edge. But now there were children and relationships to consider.

And what did the Bible say about selfishness and anger? Should they put their dreams on hold and submit to the needs and demands of aging parents?

Were there answers to such questions in any book, even the sacred pages of the Bible? Night after night, their reading lamp continued to burn.

Chapter 19 — Home

Dust sifted off the dry road and followed us to the corner as we turned toward town. Dad's green, two-door Chevrolet picked up speed as I turned to see the ranch house disappear in a brown haze.

At ten, I was old enough to know that life was taking a turn just as surely as Dad made that left-hand turn at the mailbox. The adults in my life were making some dramatic adjustments and life had already taught me that kids are just along for the ride.

The problem for me was that our house was no longer ours. It had never been ours according to Mother. It belonged to my Grandparents and they had decided it was time for us to leave.

Farm families are forward looking people. They plan and work for next year's crop all the while dreaming of one day handing the farm off to the next generation. From the youngest, picking rocks out of plowed fields, to the grandma balancing books on the kitchen table, they understand the importance of team work and pulling together. The years roll by, each one doing their part; each one, looking forward.

But then one day, the rancher and his wife are forced to deal with the reality of age and health. They grow tentative in their decisions. They lose confidence in the son or daughter that seems all too eager to take over everything they have loved and worked so hard for. Feelings get hurt, pride wounded and trust destroyed. The older generation has to provide for their golden years. The young folks, powerless and broke, can swallow their pride and stay or hit the road.

We were choosing the latter. It had taken less than ten years but now, where there had once been good will and a promising future, there was alienation and anger. And so, we were moving to town. None of us relished the idea but it seemed to be our only option.

The land that Dad and Mother had purchased earlier that spring was a long way from the Pleasant Valley School, over very bad roads. In addition to that drawback, the house had only two rooms with no running water. As parents of five kids under ten and another arriving in the fall, Mom and Dad were resigned to moving the family to a place in town.

Dad had been dreaming of his own place ever since he crossed the North Dakota, Montana line in a railroad boxcar twenty years earlier. As a boy he had watched his father go broke and lose their family farm. At sixteen he and his brothers had taken to riding the rails between Minnesota and Washington State, looking for work wherever they could find it. That's how Dad had met my grandparents. Twice, during the depression, Dad and Uncle Allen had passed through Fort Benton, both times hired by Grandpa to help with farm work. The first time, mother was married. The second time they came through, several years later, she was a widow, alone, teaching in a country school southwest of Fort Benton. By November my parents were married and the following spring, at the close of Mother's teaching contract, they moved to a highway construction site in Saltese, Montana where Dad found a truck driving job.

With the arrival of Grandpa's letter in Seattle, asking them to come home and help with the farm, Dad was eager to go in spite of Mother's objections. He wanted to do what he knew best. He wanted to farm and he wanted, someday, to have a place of his own. Perhaps this was the break he'd been hoping for.

But in spite of his best efforts, Dad always felt like a hired hand. Maybe that's the way my grandparents wanted it. Maybe they resented the fact that Mother, a college graduate, had run off with the hired help. Maybe Dad just imagined the insults he felt when Grandpa took others along to buy cattle Dad would care for or to buy equipment he would maintain and operate. Whatever the reason, Dad kept looking and hoping for a place to call his own.

The opportunity Mom and Dad had been hoping for arrived in the person of Joe Rupke. Joe, an old bachelor, was well aware of the fact that the only thing worse than a farm with a fighting family is a farm without a family. He had quietly lived on the far fringe of Pleasant Valley, never mixing much with his neighbors. But he liked Mom and Dad and one day he approached them about buying him out.

Working for board and wages, all the while raising five kids didn't allow Dad to save much money but Joe wanted my parents to have his place. He explained that he didn't have anyone to leave it to and that the place had been good to him ever since he had homesteaded there shortly after World War I. He was willing to make them a deal they couldn't refuse.

My parents could not believe their good fortune. Sealing the deal with a handshake, paperwork to follow, Dad began planning for the upcoming growing season.

Grandpa and Grandma's reaction was anger. They felt they should have been consulted. "How did he think he was going to do the work on both places?" They were certain their place would not be Dad's first priority. They were fit to be tied. Where there should have been dialog and planning, there was hostility and silence. Neither was willing to give, not even an inch.

From Mom and Dad's point of view, which is the only one I knew anything about, there were some good reasons to leave. At times they felt like they didn't get a fair shake when the calf crop was split up or the grain sold. Decisions that affected their lives were made by others. They resented the outside influence of other family members. And the ordeal of Lana's short life, so many years before, was still an open wound between my Mother and Grandmother even though the subject was always carefully avoided.

Complaints, real and imagined, reverberated from the front seat as we drove home on Sunday evenings. I didn't understand all the family dynamics, but I knew enough to know that my parents didn't enjoy our afternoons at Grandmother's house anymore.

Trapped in the back seat with my three brothers and totally bored with their nonsense and bickering, I found the conversations between Mom and Dad much more interesting but, at the same time, troubling.

It was becoming clear to me that my parents were not happy with life the way we were living it. This worried me since I thought my life was just about perfect. I thought Grandma and Grandpa were outstanding grandparents and I was sure they meant our family no ill will.

Occasionally, intent on defending my Grandparents, I would lean forward out of the tangle of male bodies and add my two cents worth.

"I don't think Grandma is mad at us," I'd offer lamely. Or, "Grandpa didn't say that." I soon learned that putting my positive spin on the events of the afternoon was not appreciated.

"You have no idea what you're talking about," Mom would tell me. "Just mind your own business and keep your opinions to yourself."

And then, reaching around to separate the boys, she reminded me not to repeat what I had been hearing.

Perhaps concerned that their complaints would find their way back to my Grandparents ears, Dad reinforced Mother's admonition. "Remember, what goes on in our family is no one else's business."

Wheat wasn't the only thing harvested that summer. Both families were reaping a bitter harvest of recriminations and betrayal. So what came next did not surprise any of us who had been paying attention.

Without consulting Mom and Dad; turn about being fair play, my Grandparents decided to get out of the farming business. The crop, cattle and equipment would be split up in the fall. The farm land and home place would be leased out to another family. We were to be moved out of the ranch house before school started.

How the adults in my life managed the next few months, I'm not sure. I know there were discussions about where we would live, about where the money was going to come from to get us settled in town, about Dad having to drive back and forth to the new place and

275

about the cash that would be needed to get his first crop in the ground.

There was very little talk with Grandma and Grandpa or even about them. Bitterness had dried up all communication just as surely as drought dries up a reservoir. Dad and Mom's focus was on getting us off the place and out of our grandparent's lives. Adding to the strain of this family feud was an unexpected pregnancy.

And it was hot. Dad wrapped up his obligations, working with Grandpa as best he could under the circumstances. Grandma stayed in town, silent and unavailable until it was time to go through all the buildings; sorting, discarding and organizing for the upcoming auction sale. Mother concentrated on packing and we kids concentrated on staying out of the way.

Sunday afternoons were now spent house hunting instead of in Grandma's cool, shady yard. With four impatient kids in the back seat and Renae in front, we cruised the searing streets of Fort Benton looking for a place that we could eventually call 'home'. Sometimes the local insurance man, who doubled as the town's lone real estate agent, would accompany us in our search, forcing all of us to be on our best behavior.

We had looked at several houses over the last few weeks; some were too small for our family and those large enough to accommodate us were beyond my parent's financial capabilities.

Collectively, we stared in dismay at the realtor's latest offering. It seemed as though all my parent's efforts had come down to this ugly excuse for a dwelling. The yard was a patch of dirt, weeds and overgrown grass, strewn with dried cottonwood branches that had, over time, crashed down around the house. Once white, the paint was now dirty gray and peeling. Broken toys, discarded furniture and worn tires littered the open spaces between the downed tree limbs.

"I don't care, Bill. I will not move into a dump like that," Mom stated emphatically. "I'll pitch a tent first."

It was late in the evening and getting dark as we sat there in the Chevrolet, light beams focused on a cracked sidewalk and torn screen door.

"We don't have a lot of choices, Jean," Dad responded, looking as tired and worn as an old pair of blue jeans. "Maybe it will look better on the inside. It's got four bedrooms. Why don't we just go in and have a look?" he coaxed.

"No," Mother snapped. "We'll just move up to Joe's." We all knew that when she made up her mind, she turned to iron. There would be no bending or softening of her position. Shrugging his shoulders, Dad put the car in reverse and backed out of the driveway.

Our headlights pulled away from the rejected property and pointed up Front Street as Dad headed towards home. Turning north we passed my grandparent's house. The lights were on in the kitchen but we knew better than to suggest stopping. Turning our eyes and hearts back towards the street, we rode home, silent, overcome by a discouragement as deep and dark as my Dad's empty pockets.

Life was suddenly back on track with a phone call. It was Dad calling from the PCA office in Great Falls

"I know, Jean. It's scary as hell. But we'll just have to pull ourselves together and do it."

The "it" Dad was referring to was the loan payment that would have to be made next fall. A brave banker at the Production Credit Association was taking a chance on a young farmer that knew the farm and ranch business and how to work hard. Betting that Dad had it in him to make a go of it on his own place, the loan officer was loaning him, not only operating money, but the down payment for a house in town.

Mother was incredulous. "I can't believe it," she said as she hung up the phone. With hope dangling in front of her like a 4th of July banner strung across Front Street, Mother was reenergized. Help had arrived at the eleventh hour, but it had arrived. With less than two weeks before school started and no place to go, she had been packing what we didn't need in boxes and stacking them on the back porch. Knowing now, that within a few days, she would have a home of her own, she attacked the remaining drawers and cupboards with determination.

The compact, stucco house on Franklin Street wasn't exactly the house she had hoped for. It would be a tight fit for our growing family with only two small bedrooms and a kitchen the size of a ship's galley. But there was a large living room, a dining room and a big basement that could be fixed up for the boys. The house had character as well as a wide, green yard, big enough to provide a place to play and a place to grow flowers. The house was sturdy and well built and best of all, it was only four blocks from the school. It would do nicely and she was happy.

But happiness never lasted very long that dismal summer. In the midst of loading furniture and boxes onto grain trucks, Mother lost the baby. Finishing the move was forgotten as Mother was rushed to the hospital. Baby Greg was born too soon and only survived long enough for my brokenhearted parents to kiss him farewell.

However, his brief visit to our world accomplished what no one else had been able to get done all summer. He helped my parents and grandparents reach across their pain and forgive each other.

There was no energy or time left for stubbornness and hard feelings. There was a baby to be buried, a family to move and five kids to be taken care of. Mom and Dad were reeling from their loss and overwhelmed with all that needed to be done.

Grandma and Grandpa needed an opportunity to express their remorse and love. Grandma's 'take charge' personality, usually resented, was now welcomed as she directed Grandpa and the boys to the ranch. While they finished loading our belongings at that end, Grandma and I helped with the unloading at the other end, putting things away as best we knew how. Aunt Dawn pitched in by taking care of Renae during the busy days that followed.

That sense of 'family' that I had been missing so desperately returned as we worked together, a team once again. Needing both my parents and grandparents, I was thankful that the barriers had come down, and for the first time in months I no longer had to worry about the people I loved the most hurting each other.

The boys and I watched as Dad waved the last pickup load out of the yard. With Mom still recovering in the hospital, it was now up to us to walk through the empty ranch house, checking for any overlooked toys, kitchen utensils, or lost socks.

Helping Dad sweep up the house while the boys hauled broken and discarded junk to the garbage barrels out back, we worked our way through the bedrooms, the front room and kitchen. Reaching the backdoor, we placed our brooms and the dustpan in the corner of the porch.

"Well, Kareen, I think that does it," Dad announced as we took one last look into the silent, empty kitchen. Reaching in, he grabbed the doorknob and pulled the backdoor closed behind us. With the same unwavering certainty, he turned, stepped out onto the rickety back steps and opened another chapter in our lives.

Leaving the only home I had ever known, should have, under normal circumstances, brought me to tears. But Dad's promise, to pick up Mom at the hospital on the way back to our new house, focused my heart on the future rather than the past.

Instead, sporting a confident smile, I slipped my hand into Dad's as I tried, unsuccessfully, to match his long strides to the car. Calling the boys to pile in the backseat, sorting out whose turn it was to sit by the windows and finally starting the engine, Dad made a wide u-turn in front of the shop, passed the ranch house and headed for home.

Family Photographs

1949 family photograph:
Denny, Dad, Jim, Kareen,
Mom and Butch

Christmas 1950: Jim, Butch,
Kareen, Mom, Renae and
Denny

Mom, Kareen, Butch, Jim
and Dad

Grandma & Grandpa with
cousin Vicky

Kareen, Denny and Butch

Denny, Butch and
Kareen

Cousin Roy, Butch and
Grandpa

Denny on Trixie

Butch and Kareen in front of
the screened porch

Denny, Dad holding Renae, Jim and cousin Billy

Kareen, Denny and Butch

First day of school

The cousins in town clothes

The cousins in Grandma's kitchen

Great
Grandma
Stellman
and family

About the Author

Kareen Bratt has lived with a lifelong disappointment; unable to claim that she was "born and raised" in Montana, since her parents drove across the border into Idaho, to the closest hospital, for her birthing.

But raised she was, on the prairies of Eastern Montana, next to the Missouri River, awash in the history of homesteading, steamboats, Lewis and Clark and the early days of the state. She and her Midwest husband have lived and worked most of their married life in Western Montana, within view of the mountains of Glacier Park and Flathead Lake. They are the parents of three grown children, eight grandchildren and three great-grandchildren.